Journey
OF THE Self
MEMOIR OF AN ARTIST

RUTH PONIARSKI

Copyright © 2020 by Ruth Poniarski

ISBN: 978-1-7347075-5-7

Edited by: Beth Crosby, Allie Coker, and Holly Lopez

Front Cover: *Journey of the Self* acrylic on canvas by Ruth Poniarski
Back Cover: *The Fortune Teller* acrylic on canvas by Ruth Poniarski

Warren
publishing

Published by Warren Publishing
Charlotte, NC
www.warrenpublishing.net
Printed in the United States

Dedicated to Mom and Dad,
George, and my unknown heroes.

Journey of the Self acrylic on canvas by Ruth Poniarski.

Journey of the Self

I sail between two worlds
Between the 'one' that I know
and the place that I fear
In search of a passage
the next expectation
To whom I am and will become
I hold myself (the modern one) and
the one who brought me here (the historical one)
Resolving the conflict of questions
that are born
Waiting for my renewal as the
old self sheds
circling the womb of time
I succumb to the journey
entering the threshold
which will lead me from myself
To the next frontier
where the answers lie
Together we sail the crest
and ride the wave
Acknowledging our purpose
We sail to a new end.

CHAPTER 1

I was so busy talking at Joseph's party, which took place in his well-lit apartment adorned with country decor, I forgot to eat. The festive celebration was a respite from the depressing situation at my apartment in the post-industrial college town.

My two roommates wanted our apartment to themselves. I felt like the third wheel taking up space as their friendship deepened. Both girls were surviving the grueling, fourth-year architecture program. I imagined they were colluding with the landlord, an elderly man who lived on the second floor, to get rid of me.

I felt like I was ten years old and back at camp, when my friend Jane and I were ostracized by my bunkmates. We were afraid to sleep at night for fear of falling victim to their pranks. The counselor was unaware, and I was afraid to tell her, so I pleaded with my parents to take me home, but they told me to stick it out. Two weeks of hell and a feeling of being plotted against lingered in my mind for many years.

The guests, all doctoral students, abandoned the party, leaving me alone with Joseph and his roommate, Willem. I wandered into Joseph's bedroom, which was adjacent to the living room, where he made a shy gesture to have sex. I gently pushed him aside because I still missed my boyfriend, Jack, who had not returned to college that semester. Jack was the one I had finally decided to grow old with, and then he'd abandoned me, leaving me alone and estranged from my peers in the architecture program. I was struggling to complete my degree but failing in my efforts.

Furthermore, I felt guilty about my past sexual experiences. These feelings had haunted me since my childhood when I played a perverted game of "doctor and patient" with a neighbor, Neil. When we were both six, I allowed Neil to inspect my body. Those feelings and senses aroused me as I experienced premature womanhood. I felt dirty and feared being discovered, prompting worries about possible promiscuity later in life.

Joseph offered me a piece of succulent, brownie cake, which I practically inhaled. That's when I realized I hadn't eaten anything since lunch. It tasted delicious, but moments later I felt dizzy and began hallucinating. I saw a landscape of lit, white candles in a darkened cell. I wondered what was happening. Was this the death of me? Suddenly, the candles disappeared, and I veered toward the window. I tried to jump, but Joseph held me back. He meekly whispered into my ear that the brownie was laced with angel dust. He looked guilty; he clearly hadn't expected me to react so drastically. He also said Professor

Kern's wife had prepared the cake, shifting the blame for his irresponsible behavior.

Angel dust, known as PCP, is a tranquilizer for large animals such as elephants and causes more drastic reactions than LSD. The floor swirled around me as I inched my way closer to the window. I needed to jump and run and let go of everything and end my misery. The window was a symbol of freedom, a passage to eternity, a path leading away from my distraught, illusory world. Joseph blocked me with all his might. I guess he never imagined such a crazy situation would develop from giving me the brownie cake. In retrospect, Joseph was deliberate and eager to offer me the brownie. He thought that by eating it, I would stray from my anxious world and succumb to his long-awaited desires: sex, sex, and more sex. That didn't happen. He guarded me from jumping for an hour before the effects wore off, then he dismissed me to my apartment.

I found my little, yellow vehicle where I had parked it. I felt safe in the familiar surroundings of my car. I started to drive and kept driving. I did not return to my apartment. Instead, I drove aimlessly, fueled by panic and paranoia. My brain fed me lies. Suddenly, I believed a revolution was taking place in America. The socialists were in a civil war against the capitalists, and the Jewish population was leaving Earth in spaceships. I felt abandoned because I wasn't informed where the spaceships were. I could not flee to my home on Long Island because my parents would be on the spaceships. Where could I find solace and peace and escape from the plethora of imagined anguish and human failure, the downfall of my existence?

I drove eastward, then turned around and drove westward, reaching the New York State Thruway. I entered the highway and proceeded south, hoping to reach Jack's brother, who was attending college about an hour and a half away. He could help me escape the revolution and locate the spaceships. I kept driving late into the night, and I became frantic, unsure, and physically anxious. A doubt bombarded my warped mind. What if Jack's brother *couldn't* help me? What if he had already escaped Earth just to get away from me? I turned around and commenced driving north in a frenzy. In a flash, I changed my direction again. Maybe Jack's brother *could* help me? Again and again I changed my direction.

Finally, I drove to the shoulder of the thruway and parked my car. I got out and started walking southward on the shoulder of the desolate highway. It was after midnight. I purposely discarded my purse so no one would discover who I was. I could create a new identity. I could be someone else. I continued to walk with frenetic energy. I walked through a wet, swampy area and lost my shoes. Maybe Jack's brother *could* help me? I kept walking in his direction until the early dawn, oblivious to any cars swooshing by and insensitive to the cold, damp earth around me. When the sun started to rise, I walked away from the highway and veered toward a hilly road that led me to a convenience store.

Abruptly, I stopped walking and hesitated to enter the shop. My reluctance abated when a burly, African American man around thirty years old emerged from the store and walked toward his grayish, nondescript van. He glanced at me, and I glanced at him. He asked me if I needed a ride.

I paused, then agreed to his offer. I stepped into the van and noticed sleeping quarters in the back and a big rifle suspended on the side wall. I was calm when he made a nonverbal gesture, inviting me to engage in a sexual affair. I replied that I was not well and had to urinate. Then I stepped out of the van, hid behind it, and relieved my bladder. I got back into the van, and this mysterious man, whom I instantly trusted, started driving northward toward my apartment.

As we traveled a quiet road, the man posed questions in a kind attempt to discern what was troubling me. He asked me if I played the piano. I eagerly responded that I not only played the piano, but I also painted. He avoided questions about my family or school. He graciously responded to my answers by saying he wouldn't mind if I became his wife. I was bedraggled, but I did not smell of liquor or have any needle marks on my arms. My speech was clear of any nasal congestion. To him, I suppose I was a clean, white girl who had very little dignity left.

We were approaching my apartment when this kind stranger stopped his vehicle. I was overwhelmed with the dim reality of returning to my depressing apartment. As I left the van, I invited him to my apartment as my guest. He turned down my invitation because he feared that anyone at my apartment (possibly the police) would question and condemn him since he was black. He knew people would be waiting for me to reappear.

Who knew if this man's rifle ownership was legal or if he had a home or lived in his van? Whatever his truth entailed, he would be stereotyped and condemned for the innocent kindness he bestowed upon me. I thanked him for his compassionate efforts and walked the rest of the way to my apartment on sore, tired feet. My mind was in a haze as I passed cars that looked familiar, but I couldn't quite place them. I climbed the steps that led to my ground-floor apartment and opened the unlocked door. A den full of people anxiously awaited my return. Joseph, Willem, my roommates, and my bewildered father were all there. My father struggled to keep himself together.

Fears of gigantic proportions had surfaced when the perplexed state police discovered my car abandoned on the shoulder of the New York State Thruway. My father told me the state police had called his office and informed him of my abandoned car and said they found writings nestled in the rear of the car. They interpreted the writings as revolutionary, and they believed I was a rebellious dissident like Patty Hearst. The writings were assignments from Professor Kern's class. He lectured on socialism in architecture and theories he developed that coincided with that form of political organization.

Everyone looked shocked by my shoeless feet, disheveled hair, and soiled clothes. I cringed with embarrassment. In my stupor, I blocked out everyone because I didn't trust their concerns and false sincerity. I did not believe they truly cared for my well-being. They continued to stare at me. I noticed my father trying to hold back tears. I was evasive about where I had been and just kept repeating that I had a magical experience in the past twenty-four hours. Being surrounded by this small crowd in my cramped apartment kept me from running away again.

I continued to be vague. After all, I did not know anything about this considerate man who brought me back to my dismal world. I did not know his name or where he lived. He remained a kind and caring stranger who appeared casually in my life. I told my father that I hitched a ride back to my apartment. He didn't pry or ask me any questions. He didn't challenge my vague explanation. He was just content that I was alive.

We gathered my belongings, which weren't much as I practically lived out of my suitcase, and went to the local Holiday Inn for the night. I never returned to my dismal apartment again. My devoted father and I had dinner at the hotel. I found the food to be exceptional, since I hadn't eaten in more than twenty-four hours. My hunger distracted me from thoughts of the "revolution." All I could think about was my ravenous appetite and devouring the food before me.

My father stayed awake all night to ensure I didn't run away again. We had one tender moment when I told my father that I had really made a mess of things. I reached out of my psychotic dungeon briefly, then flipped back into delusions, imagining I was Jesus and going to be persecuted by millions of earthlings. My mind raced with uncontrollable punitive thoughts, keeping me from falling into a deep slumber. Instead, I lay frozen on the bed in a panicky, motionless state of fear, watching the reflections of headlights on the wall across from my bed. I believed the lights were from spaceships transporting earthlings. I had to escape, but I couldn't move, and my father had no idea what I was imagining. He couldn't convince me that all was safe. I was immersed in an irrational world disconnected from any reasonable semblance of reality and sanity.

Meanwhile, my father desperately attempted to reach a psychiatrist near our home on Long Island. Dad was panic-stricken when he couldn't reach Dr. Samuels. There was no escaping this perilous situation, and my father feared the worst scenario—that I would run away again and never be found.

The following morning, we exited the college town that would leave a hollow place in my heart. My father was still frightened about bringing me home. He kept one hand on me and his other hand on the steering wheel. The convenience of cell phones did not exist in 1977, so my father had to stop at numerous gas stations along the New York State Thruway to call Dr. Samuels on public phones. His fear and anxiety were insurmountable. At any moment I could break away and jump out of the car. Dad said that was the most difficult journey in his life other than when he was a soldier in World War II.

CHAPTER 2

Dad miraculously kept me intact, and we finally arrived at the doctor's office. We waited in an area by the front entrance.

In my irrational state of mind, I was afraid of talking to the doctor. This form of "medicine," addressing mental illness, was stigmatized in the 1970s. The medical field had limited clinical experience to offer patients like me.

As I waited with unsettling anticipation, my imagined "revolution" took a back seat. I was so remorseful that I had disappointed my parents, especially my mother, who was so gorgeous and refined. I believed I could never meet her standards of beauty. I felt unattractive and undesirable, always walking in her shadow.

Dr. Samuels finally opened his office door. He looked like Moses straight out of the Bible. He had a beard, was slightly bald, and wore wire-framed eye glasses. Dad remained in the waiting area. He appeared relieved but also a bit nervous, quietly tapping his foot as I entered the office of this unfamiliar doctor. Dr. Samuels seemed like someone to consult, but I was skeptical and not ready to share my mind. Instead, I reverted back to the "revolution" that was haunting my psyche, and I wanted to escape.

For about twenty minutes, cold silence filled the air. Perhaps the doctor was trying to gain my trust. He didn't inquire about any events preceding my breakdown. Dr. Samuels practiced Freudian therapy and rarely said anything. If he had spoken on his own life experiences or shared anecdotes, I would have felt more comfortable. His silence intensified my feelings of being an outcast, an inadequate woman who thought everyone was superior to her.

A perplexing photograph hung on the wall above the couch where patients lay. The dull image consisted of an eagle's wing in the upper left corner. Below it was a bare landscape with a line of telephone poles evenly spaced apart and connected by electrical wires.

This bleak picture disturbed me because it played into my feelings of isolation. When I was a toddler, Mom and Dad had always completely closed the door to my room at bedtime, and the resulting dark space would engulf me while I struggled to sleep. I felt abandoned by my parents.

Dr. Samuels informed my father that I had experienced a nervous breakdown and could convalesce at home instead of a psych ward—a place I feared the most, where I would be locked up for eternity, further abandoned by humanity. I envisioned the ward's rooms to be lonely cells at an institution like the one portrayed in the movie *One Flew Over the Cuckoo's Nest*. The doctor prescribed Thorazine, the recommended antipsychotic drug at the time.

I suppose Dad was anxious about how Mom would react and the events that might follow. My mother knew my youth was plagued with stressful situations, but she was helpless in recognizing the subtlety of destructive forces and my predisposition to mental illness.

My parents and I communicated sparsely. They came from households where few nurturing words were expressed and were unaware of the pitfalls of our developing modern world in 1977. Sexual liberation and women in the workforce were on the horizon. Mom was a traditional woman, unable to be a role model for my ambitions of becoming an architect in a male-dominated field. She had many talents, including an acumen for designing clothes and a beautiful singing voice, and she was an accomplished violinist, but she chose to be a housewife and devote her time to family.

※

Dad and I reached our final destination: home. My mother did not hug me. That was not her style. She held herself together, and underneath an iron façade, she hid her concern about the journey ahead. She wisely structured the days around meals and art projects.

I hadn't slept for two days. The "revolution" still preyed on my mind. I could not sleep because I feared waking to an abandoned world. My mind raced with berating, self-punishing thoughts emanating from an underlying guilt about my sexual experiences in college.

The Thorazine eventually induced sleep. Little by little, I began to trust the world was safe, and I slept more deeply. The "revolution" gradually faded, and hope for a promising future began to develop, although my feelings of inferiority and inadequacy lurked in my subconscious. I felt like an outsider among my peers in college, as well as in my generation, certain I was the only student in my class to face mental illness, a prevailing stigma.

I managed to complete a painting of three, large hyperrealistic apples, and Mom hung it on a prominent wall in the living room. Despite the success of this rendering, Mom advised me that being an artist was isolating, and making a living would be difficult.

※

Therapy sessions were twice weekly. I gradually spoke of my experiences, mostly about my high school years. For instance, when I was a majorette during my junior year, the captain nominated me to be the next captain, but no one in the corps supported her endorsement. I felt lonely and dejected as a result, and my self-esteem was blown away.

I described a recurring dream that haunted me since my junior year in college when I was dating Jack. I was isolated and standing in the remains of an abandoned house overlooking a desolate valley below a vast cliff. Squirrels and rats were my company as I stood frozen, peering downward at the valley of death. My hair was overgrown. My older brother, Rob, and John, an unrequited love from college, led a long line of blonde-haired women through the empty valley that was once a vibrant body of water. I longed to be with them instead of existing in my loneliness and feeling inadequate. Again, I was an outsider looking into a world where I was not accepted, feeling cursed and trapped for all eternity.

Dr. Samuels did not speak, and his notes were minimal. He relied on his memory. He preferred that his patients lie on his couch and converse freely in rambling associations, creating a window into the past. I did not feel comfortable with this method of psychotherapy. I never got to the core of what was causing my psychosis. I was afraid and embarrassed to dig deep.

After his silence, Dr. Samuels did not express any insight into how I might lead a less chaotic life by consciously developing a support system. He did not acknowledge the symptoms of my illness (such as sleep deprivation) or address my limitations, nor did he advise me to "take a day at a time" and work on small goals rather than obsessing about what would happen thirty years into the future. I feared being abandoned; I imagined I was inadequate and undesirable.

CHAPTER 3

The days passed steadily, and I nearly forgot about Jack. I didn't correspond with him because I had nothing to write about, and he lived in Belgium with his father and two brothers. His parents were divorced. Jack's mom was a news correspondent in France, putting her career over family, and his father was the highest paid American executive in Europe at the time.

One day, Jack sent me a letter. I assumed he was writing to tell me he was returning to New York to rekindle our romance. My heart fluttered with anticipation. I took a deep breath and opened the letter. As I read it, my elated emotions gushing with love plummeted over a cliff. He informed me that he was attending an architecture program in Sweden. He did not close his letter with "love," and from the tone I could tell he was over me.

I had been accepted to the Sorbonne for a year but opted instead to return to the college in the North and reenroll in design studio, a class I foolishly dropped in my junior year of the five-year program. Had I studied in France, Jack would have pursued our relationship. Attending college abroad was a pipe dream because I was unable to speak French fluently.

Had Jack returned to the States, I would have avoided my breakdown, and I would not have befriended Joseph, the instigator of my undoing. Luckily, the Thorazine had calmed my racing mind, and I was able to be rational and plan my future of returning to college.

Joseph visited me at home a few weeks later. He was a New Englander, and this was his first trip to Long Island, as he'd finally mustered the courage to explore new territory. He'd come with the sole purpose of apologizing for drugging me. At the time, I did not realize my dangerous breakdown was triggered by the angel dust, a catalyst that unleashed my predisposition to an illness of the mind.

He gave me a book titled *The Legend of Sleepy Hollow* by Washington Irving. Joseph had written a flimsy message on the inside jacket: "How Ichabod of me." His apology was referencing his stupid, headless act of giving me the angel dust. Ichabod was the name of the headless character in the story. After he left, I never heard from him again.

In the dead of winter, I worked for my father, drafting waterproofing and roofing details for prominent buildings in New York City. I fell into a dull routine, devoid of any aspirations of being the head of his company in the future. Dad did not offer any words of encouragement in that regard.

I enrolled in two architecture-related courses for the 1978 spring semester at Columbia University. I struggled when reading textbooks and writing scholarly term papers. I traveled between my father's company in Brooklyn and the city. It was tedious, but I survived.

Meeting students to befriend was a challenge since I commuted to school. I often conversed with an attractive female student who sat next to me in class. She seemed stable, studious, focused, and around my age. She was also engaged to a man ten years her senior. Her circumstances made me think that at my age of twenty-two years, I was ready to marry, but there was no viable prospect on the horizon. Eventually, I feverishly hunted for Mr. Right. Marriage was a convention I longed for.

I barely passed the two courses, though, fortunately, I was able to transfer the credits to the next architecture program I attended.

⁂

After spring term ended, I met Todd, who lived in my hometown and was a member of the community temple where we met. He was my brother's age, three years older than me. Todd had received a degree in geology, an unpopular area of study, from the same college in the North that I had attended.

Neither Todd nor his parents nor the community had knowledge of my illness. Mom and Dad did not confide in anyone because the resulting gossip would undermine our well-being. Todd was good looking and tall. He had a bland, pensive personality that minimized his appeal and presented a challenge to appreciating his kind nature. I was tentative in pursuing a relationship with Todd despite his handsome looks.

The few times Todd and I went on a date, we saw movies at the town theater during the weekdays when the audience was sparse. I felt awkward sitting in a large, silent theater not knowing what to converse about. I avoided talking about the college in the North because that was a painful memory. We always remained timid and unsure of ourselves until the movie started. I had no idea what he was thinking or feeling, and that is how it remained.

During late afternoons on weekends, I jogged at the high school track about four miles from my home. One time, as I approached the track, I saw Todd talking to a girl across the field. I felt jealous and soon realized that I had feelings for the quiet man who remained a mystery in our limited engagements. When he recognized me from afar, he ended his conversation and quickly approached me. He convinced me that the girl was an acquaintance. Then he returned home on his bicycle, and I continued running.

❈

During the summer of 1978, I worked as an assistant to a project manager at a construction site for a new Hyatt hotel in the heart of Manhattan. The project included renovating The Commodore Hotel, transforming it into a modern structure. My role was expediting the interior design of a mock-up floor that would establish the aesthetic pattern for the rest of the floors in the hotel.

I was one of the first women to be employed on a construction site in Manhattan. The project manager, a man in his thirties, often remarked that a dirty construction site was no place for a woman, and I should be working in a plush interior-design office. His words put a damper on my hopes because my passion was elsewhere, waiting to be ignited. I was just filling my time in a career I was settling on. Luckily, I did not work directly with the construction crews. It would have been impossible to enforce any supervision because the male laborers were accustomed to taking orders from foremen.

Architects were notorious for making mistakes in their construction documents—the instructions on how to build a viable design. The general contractor for whom I worked and the subcontractors who provided roofing, electrical, steel, HVAC, and so forth often had to step in and correct errors. There were so many considerations in renovating a building that it was a daunting task to be consistently accurate.

The original exterior of the hotel was brick exterior, but it was now covered by a reflective glass wall, which converted the building into a glitzy edifice. The construction office was on the twentieth floor, where the project manager and I were based. The day started at 8:30 a.m. and ended at 4:00 p.m.

Renovating the hotel took two years. I was tempted to remain at the job during the entire project instead of returning to architecture school, but I was obstinate and determined to finish what I had started in 1974. Regardless of my inner turmoil and the notion that this direction was a wrong path not practical for my talents, I decided to attend another architecture program in the fall.

✤

Todd visited me at the construction site, and the men teased me that Robert Redford was there to see me; for a second, I thought they spoke the truth. I was astonished to see him and totally amazed that he was interested in my summer endeavor. He looked so handsome wearing a suit and tie. I was sure I was one of many women who wanted to date him.

Despite his looks, Todd was reserved and unsure of himself. Like me, he was going through the motions of living, void of any passion, lost, passive, and floundering for a meaningful direction. These feelings persisted despite the reality that we had careers and that our time was filled with practical pursuits.

Todd left shortly after arriving. He was on his way to a job interview. The next time I saw him was when I visited his home on the other side of town. In the heat of the summer, we went swimming in the backyard pool. We were quiet as usual, so I broke the silence by talking about an incident from my youth. My family dog, Scamper, a large German Shepherd, had abruptly jumped upward. As I rose from the couch in the den of my home, he landed on my cheek, cutting it open. I was only six years old and freaked out because blood was oozing down my face. My mother placed a cloth drenched with liquor on my open wound to disinfect it, and I was traumatized by the sharp pain. Dad took me to the hospital emergency room, and a cosmetic surgeon closed my face with stiches. This horrific event had marred my innocent youth, and I blamed myself for what had happened to me. Todd said that it was mature of me to take responsibility for the accident, but it seemed like he was judging me. I failed to realize he was trying to keep a dialogue.

We were searching for a common thread between our downtrodden souls. Yet in the back of my mind lurked the dark secret of my breakdown and the fear that if he found out he would reject me. This initiated my living a double life. One side of me sustained shallow friendships and an appearance of normalcy, and the other side was owned by my hidden psychosis.

Following my visit to Todd's house, I began to experience feelings of being alone. I felt disassociated and divorced from myself. My demons were surfacing. I was hanging on the edge of a cliff. My nerves were fragile, and my mind was consumed with thoughts of a barren future with everyone gone. I imagined being abandoned and doomed to life in a desolate world.

During this time, Todd and I saw a movie. I was silent, holding myself by a thread, hoping Todd would not notice my compromised behavior. The movie was violent and titled *The Deer Hunter*. One of the main characters dies from playing Russian roulette with a gun at a dingy club in Vietnam following the war. The turbulent story resonated deep within me and brought the festering fears of my bleak, lonely existence to the foreground. I became desperate. I asked Todd if he would marry me and start a new life in California, thinking that my demons would disappear forever.

I never alluded to the reason why I wanted to move to California, and Todd was sullen and calm as he said he would think about it.

CHAPTER 4

My demons subsided for the moment, but deep inside, I fought a battle with loneliness. Todd never answered my proposal, and because of our respective mental strife, we failed to connect on a deeper level, always struggling for conversation. He was so close yet so far away. Though Todd probably maintained a cool distance from people in his life, I took it personally. I was betrayed by Joseph, rejected by Jack, and emotionally stranded by Todd.

Before I was involved with Jack, I dated a fifth-year architecture student, or "archie," named Roy. During the spring term of my sophomore year at the college in the North, we were in the heat of a burgeoning relationship, visiting my parents and his family, taking a trip to Provincetown, Massachusetts, and so forth. Despite us being together, I could not connect emotionally or appreciate Roy's romantic efforts. I attribute this to the heavy marijuana smoking I'd done before I met him. It made me feel listless and detached, and feelings of inadequacy surfaced. My studies suffered, and I barely passed. Furthermore, I was romantically obsessed about a student, John, who I believed was a genius in design class. He was a deep thinker, and all my peers revered him. One day I found out the underlying reason for John's pensive, mysterious demeanor. His father and brother committed suicide. I could have helped him cope with his deepening depression, but he did not want to burden me with problems I was unaware of at the time. My relationship with Roy never developed as I dwelled on the impossible prospect of dating John (before I met Jack).

⁂

Roy graduated and abandoned me when he returned to Buffalo, New York, to continue his life. There was no closure of words between us. He just left me behind. I felt rejected and not good enough despite my detachment. My unresolved feeling of inadequacy loomed, perpetuating a burden within.

⁂

One weekend in the summer, Vinny, another archie from my class in the North, visited me at my home. I did not know him well, but he was persistent in pursuing a long-distance affair. He visited intermittently throughout a decade while I dated other men.

Vinny was a tall, good-looking, Asian man. He drove a dingy, nondescript van that had a bed behind the driver's seat. As I became familiar with him, I discovered he was too strongly opinionated and ambitious to be successful in the architecture world. I always wondered whether Vinny knew about my breakdown. He never mentioned it, and I don't think he cared.

Vinny also dated a buxom, blond-haired woman, Gail, in the North. She was bisexual, and in addition to being a student, Gail was a stripper at a bar. Vinny warned me that she was jealous because he was pursuing me. Gail eventually quit being a stripper and focused on studying to be a successful gynecologist.

Luckily, Gail didn't know where I lived, so any confrontation was avoided. Vinny and I decided to embark on a road trip to eastern Long Island in his van. During the trip, I started to menstruate, and I had thoughtlessly left my sanitary napkins at home. It was late in the night, and we couldn't find any store that was open. My blood was everywhere, and I became desperate. I treated Vinny shabbily, and I was embarrassed. In the morning, we drove back to my home, and I rushed out of the van to take a much-needed shower. The crisis was over, and I was clean again. Vinny was upset with my behavior, and I pleaded for his forgiveness. After a few hours, he returned to the North. I think Vinny was hesitant to continue our friendship after witnessing my unpleasant side.

I was treading the murky waters to stay afloat while everyone around me had their agendas, finding a direction and gaining clarity. I was floundering and remiss in planning my future or establishing goals. I was afraid to break away from architecture and seek another path that I found to be a little less challenging and closer to my heart, such as the fine arts. My mother swayed me and stressed that painting was an isolating profession. In retrospect, I should have sought a graduate degree in art at Yale University.

My carelessness manifested in my failure to plan each day, problem solve effectively, and consciously keep myself from spiraling into another breakdown. Though surrounded by people, I felt desperately alone, with the demons in my mind.

The summer of 1978 came to an end, and I bid farewell to the project manager at the construction site. Fall arrived, and I attended an architecture program in the heart of Brooklyn. I carried my internal burdens—fears that my peers might learn of my psychotic side, that I might be conspicuous in my thoughts of failure and not being accepted. However, I tackled a full schedule of courses.

The architecture building where most of the classes met was an old structure in need of renovation. The campus was small compared to the college in the North. The college in Brooklyn specialized in fine arts and architecture and offered a minimal engineering program.

I soon learned that most of the students commuted from Manhattan, and I would drive to the college each day in my little, yellow car. I dressed in skirts and jackets, and I stood out from the crowd because most students wore T-shirts and jeans. I marched to my own beat and was on a mission to attract a man. I tended to that specific goal and put my education in second place. I forgot about my unresolved relationships while discovering new ground to explore, and no one had any knowledge of my past.

I could have easily channeled my energy into painting, but I was stubbornly committed to architecture, the more difficult path. I was determined to find a soul mate ... and maybe succeed in my studies while I was at it.

My first project included designing a modular house, a prototype that integrated heating and cooling to define the form of the structure. I installed my drafting desk in the corner of my bedroom. I was in a place I needed to be, the comfort and stability of homelife, which made it feasible to focus on my studies without any distractions.

Deena, a friend from summer camp days in my youth, visited my home in early fall 1978 after I finally established a study routine. She was an achiever, having earned a bachelor's degree in fine arts and criminology with high honors. She invited me to move to New York City and be roommates in an apartment. The thought of living in the city as a single woman was enticing. The importance of having a stable haven at my home diminished because I was easily convinced by Deena and the infinite social opportunities that would surface while living in the city. I did not consider that I would have to commute to Brooklyn by subway and establish a stable study regimen amid the distractions of the city environment.

Mom didn't like Deena and didn't approve of me sharing an apartment with her. I should have listened to my mother's warnings of pursuing an uneven friendship tainted with rivalry.

Deena was always jealous of my hourglass figure and creativity. My mother was aware of an underlying animosity that Deena subtly showed toward me. I was blind to it at the time because I always admired Deena for her beautiful, golden hair and bright blue-green eyes and for having read many authors.

Deena and I searched all over the city. We could barely afford a one-bedroom apartment. I also explored on my own during the day because Deena worked full-time for an upscale clothing company in the city. I found a beautiful studio apartment on the upper east side and considered it for myself, but I was afraid to live alone.

We continued our search and discovered a one-bedroom apartment on the lower east side of Manhattan. It was on the seventh floor of a building that once housed offices. Deena and I argued about who would get the bedroom and who would create a room from part of the living room space.

Deena grew impatient, and she shouted at me, "What do you want?"

I cowered, intimidated by her psychological game. I timidly chose the living room. We should have picked a number out of a hat. That would have been democratic, and Deena should have offered to pay a higher rent since she had the better space. We moved into the apartment in October 1978.

The ceiling height was twelve feet. I decided to build an eight-foot wall dividing the living room to create a private space with windows that faced the street. Vinny and one of my father's employees built the wall in a day.

Vinny was a loyal friend who wanted me to be happy in my new space. He traveled far, but I took him for granted. Looking back, I should have given him a gift for his generous efforts.

Deena spent most of her time in her bedroom after a full day of work, and I toiled on my design projects at a drafting desk I had installed against the wall opposite my bed.

One day, when I was standing on the subway platform while commuting to the Brooklyn campus, I glanced across the track and noticed a handsome man who looked like an actor. He was a student in my class, and eventually I would meet him. Like me, he dressed impeccably and had a graceful posture. Fate was playing a game with me. My aspirations to find a man might be realized, and I began to feel a subtle connection to this stranger.

Meanwhile, Deena maintained her job at the prestigious clothing company. She created advertising layouts, organized photo shoots of models, and so forth. She had to be creative, and she sought my opinion. I seldom remarked, however, because I didn't want her to know I found her layouts appealing. I was surprised that she approached me for advice. I felt I lagged behind her in everything. She had graduated with honors and was on her way to establishing herself in the workforce. I had a long road, two more years, to complete the architecture program. Had she been a student like me, commuting to college, our relationship would have been based on more common ground, working toward the same goal.

Before Deena and I moved into our apartment, I befriended Bill, a fellow archie I met in design class. He was my height, good-looking, and preppy. He came from a wealthy family. His father owned a high-rise building in Stanford, Connecticut, as well as a mansion in New Canaan, Connecticut. Bill was living in his father's gorgeous apartment in Manhattan on the upper east side.

Bill invited me to go sailing with him, his sister, his mother, and her second husband. Bill's stepfather owned an impressive boat and demonstrated sharp sailing skills, navigating the winds and strong currents of the Long Island Sound.

That glorious day in September made me nostalgic and stirred appreciation in my soul. While casually conversing, Bill revealed to me that he recently shed a lot of weight and was feeling good about his success in slimming down. Having just met him, I was slightly startled that he was so candid about his personal struggles.

Following a full afternoon of sailing, Bill took his sister and me to their father's house in New Canaan. I was impressed with the palatial mansion of beautiful rooms. No doubt the home was arranged with the expertise of an interior designer. I carefully followed Bill, and we ascended a grand staircase to his second-floor bedroom.

I showered in Bill's bathroom, got dressed, and applied some makeup. He then led me into his brother's bedroom, which was connected by a common door. I sat on the edge of his brother's bed, feeling awkward, while Bill and his sister smoked marijuana. My memories of my sordid past kept me from partaking. I felt like the odd man, and the peer pressure was daunting, but I was adamant in declining. The good vibes from the day's activities were lost. Following the drug interlude, Bill and I went downstairs, where he introduced me to his authoritative father and his Southern belle girlfriend who were eating in the formal dining room. The girlfriend commented on my Polish name. Her offensive attitude startled me, and I was perplexed by the father's choice of mate after spending the day with Bill's charming and beautiful mother.

Bill and I left the house and drove to a fine restaurant for dinner. My jittery nerves from meeting his family for the first time subsided as I sipped a glass of wine and finally enjoyed being alone with Bill. We both reveled in the day spent together, and I believed our brief encounter could blossom into a meaningful relationship. After dinner, Bill and I returned to his father's house.

Bill wanted me to stay the night. It was eleven o'clock, and I decided to return home. He pleaded with me not to travel so late, but I was determined to leave. I hardly knew him, and he wanted to get too close too soon. I was embarrassed to think we could have developed a relationship with conservative boundaries. Bill thought he could buy me with his affluence. I escaped compromising myself.

I reluctantly invited Bill to dinner at my apartment shortly after Deena and I moved in. I covered the small dining table against the wall opposite the living room with a pink sheet and then placed a little candle in the center of the table. I made pasta with meat sauce, my specialty. Bill arrived not knowing what to expect since I declined to have sex on our first date.

As we sat at the intimate table sipping wine, Deena made her entrance and complimented the dinner I prepared. She did not know how to cook. I noticed Bill was instantly drawn to Deena's vivid blue-green eyes. In that painful moment, I felt like Deena was reveling in the attention meant to be mine.

I felt my efforts to create a romantic evening dissolve. When Deena retired to her bedroom, Bill and I resumed our dinner with little enthusiasm. It seemed to me the highlight of Bill's evening had disappeared.

He left shortly after eating dinner. I was disappointed and suspected I would never see him again outside of class. The initial novelty between us dissipated after I acknowledged his immaturity when he realized I wanted more than a physical relationship. I said goodbye to his world and sailed onward, searching for other prospects.

CHAPTER 5

The bedroom I created from the living room space featured a wall of windows facing the street. I often opened a window to refresh the stillness of my bedroom. I cherished the brisk wind and chill in the air. They stirred memories from when Mom and Dad had taken my brother Rob and me on ski trips to southern Vermont, where I had the opportunity to brave nature. Sometimes the windchill factor was below zero when we skied there, but I enjoyed the company of Dad and Rob and being surrounded by a small crowd of ski enthusiasts. Mom chose not to ski because she was afraid of breaking her legs.

In the beginning of those winter adventures, my mother had dressed her five-year-old daughter and eight-year-old son in unflattering ski attire. Nylon shell pants bunched up at my knees, invoking a chubby appearance. They were practical for insulating our legs and shielding us from the cold, but I was disappointed. I yearned to be pretty. Rob and I were the only skiers wearing those unattractive pants. At a young age, in the beginning of elementary school, I had always felt ugly because all my female peers had long hair and I had short hair, which my mother kept cutting and styling. Then, when I was nine years old and attending a local summer camp, I befriended a fellow camper, Lori, who had short hair. I had grown out my hair, and she was jealous. When we were visiting her male friend outside of camp, she called me ugly and I believed her. Because I felt so ugly, I wanted to dress like my peers, but my mother's taste in clothing differed from the trends of the day; my clothes were always dated and lacking in style. I struggled with feelings of being different and unattractive.

⁂

One night at my drafting desk, I was working on a challenging assignment—the design of a subway entrance. I kept myself alert by opening the window. Suddenly, Deena barged into my room and abruptly closed the window, claiming it was too cold. Shortly after her rude outburst, Danny, a close friend of her boyfriend, Monte, came into my bedroom from the living room. Danny was an architect, and he flattered me on the complexity of my design for the subway entrance. I was attracted to Danny and his warm, engaging personality. Sadly, he was not available. He was dating Deena's friend, an architecture student at Columbia University.

I felt alone, struggling for some peace, excluded from Deena's clique. I was certain a connection existed between Danny and me, but he was roped into Deena's rivalrous world.

Monte was a successful businessman earning an impressive salary. He worked in the city and frequently made trips to the South. He was tall, blond, and rugged like the Marlboro Man. Monte stored his clothes in Deena's closet. Without my approval, he was moving into our apartment inch by inch at no cost. I was afraid to confront him and demand that he share the cost of rent. I felt like I was being taken advantage of, and Deena couldn't have cared less.

In November 1978, while Monte was traveling, Deena confided in me she was pregnant, and he had told her to abort the pregnancy. I was surprised when Deena asked me to accompany her to Planned Parenthood.

I remember helping Deena climb in the Sinai Desert during a trip with Ramah Camp to Israel in the summer of 1972. A group of thirty American high-school students ascended Mt. Sinai at 3:00 a.m. before the intense sunrise and the heat of the day was upon us.

Deena was walking in front of me when she fell and wounded her knee. She complained like a baby. I helped her up from the arid ground, and she leaned on me for the remainder of the climb along a narrow path. She never thanked me for the assistance I had provided as a caring friend.

I escorted Deena to Planned Parenthood to comfort her. Deena told me about her pregnancy, because she knew deep down I was honorable and would never betray her trust. She took advantage of my character in every way.

Since Monte was absent, I wondered if the end of their relationship was near. However, when Monte returned to New York, they resumed their bond as if nothing had happened. They were stronger than ever, brushing me to the side. Deena never thanked me for my support, and she resumed her animosity toward me.

Soon Monte's business no longer required traveling. He had moved into our apartment as a full-time tenant, and I was livid. This was not the scenario I imagined. Again, I felt like the third wheel. I couldn't control my anger, and it was overwhelming.

I should have packed my things and moved back home. Instead I was passive and unable to seek resolution. As time slowly passed, anger clouded my vision. I began to believe people were conspiring against me. I became withdrawn and unable to move forward. I was certain that Deena would be pleased to see me fail.

My anger deepened, and I couldn't sleep for days. I barely passed the semester. At night, when I was tossing and turning with racing, uncontrollable thoughts, I gazed at the façade of the buildings across the street. I hallucinated that the gargoyles on the window cornices looked like Jesus. The bearded faces glared at me throughout the night. I felt desperately alone and unwelcome. I screamed within, and no one could hear me. I had a surge of energy that accompanied my frenzied emotions, and I attempted to build a lofted bed by using the remaining wood from the wall I had built. I hammered beam-ends into the wall, but I didn't have enough lumber to complete the bed. Morning arrived without any slumber or sense of completion for me.

In the morning, Monte peered into my bedroom and spouted words that I was sexually attracted to my father. Such an accusation was absurd and made me more panic-stricken. He made that disturbing remark as a ploy to get rid of me. Any hope of having a positive existence in the city plummeted. This was war. The devious couple didn't care what happened to me.

I didn't leave the apartment for days. To broker peace, I asked Deena to sign a document stating that we lived on separate sides of the apartment and Monte should contribute to the rent. I gently apologized for being uncooperative about Monte moving in. She fiercely declared that only a fool would sign. Her harsh tone made me cower. I was ineffective in settling our disagreement, and I became more despondent.

I sat on the couch in our small living room, strumming my guitar. I was searching for an answer to my unestablished life. Perhaps I could become a singer, and my struggle to become an architect would fade. I could begin anew. I could be a star.

Deena and Monte were passing through the living room when she casually mentioned I should play "The Sound of Silence" by Simon and Garfunkel, which begins with talk of darkness. Her suggestion spurred my fragmented mind, and I saw myself blind and trapped in a black void of death. I interpreted the title of the song literally in my confused state. Her taunts were purposeful. Then Monte maliciously joked that I should turn to drinking alcohol. They had no compassion for me or recognition that I was breaking down.

I had no one to turn to, even though I was seeing Dr. Samuels twice a week. He believed my troubles stemmed from separation issues with my mother and recommended I limit being dependent on my parents. He advised me to seek support from strangers and establish independence, but that was not happening. I gradually avoided my sessions with Dr. Samuels. He couldn't acknowledge my crisis and the pattern of psychosis developing. In sessions, I pretended to be stable, afraid I would be locked up in a psych ward while darkness devoured me. My world was broken into a million insane pieces.

My anger reached a breaking point as I no longer could contain myself. I marched into Deena's room in the middle of the night to confront her. Monte was sitting on the edge of the bed, completely naked, but he grabbed me and held me back. Deena looked afraid, shielding her face with her hands; perhaps she believed I was dangerous. There was fear in her eyes while she cowered on her side of the bed, and she became nastier in her comments.

I don't remember who called my father that night, but he came to the apartment the following day. We packed my belongings and left an impossible situation. Monte and Deena had the apartment to themselves.

CHAPTER 6

After he rescued me from Deena and Monte, my father took me to Dr. Samuels. My session with the doctor did not help my condition. The psychiatrist never acknowledged that Deena had wronged me, and he failed to point out that the layman has no understanding of my illness. Deena and Monte could not recognize that I was breaking down. They just enacted war to achieve their goal of getting rid of me.

The doctor didn't realize the pattern of psychosis developing when a stressful situation evolved. My illness was difficult to understand and not defined in the same way as diabetes or a heart condition. His Freudian style of therapy was not effective in curtailing my decompensation. I needed him to tell me the basics for my survival within the boundaries of my limitations. I needed to know that I should avoid chaos and too many events happening at once. He should have warned me against reenrolling in an architecture program and making a big move into the city at the same time. Dr. Samuels said I could convalesce at home again. And he once again prescribed Thorazine. I had not slept for days, and the prescribed dosage wasn't strong enough to induce sleep immediately.

When night arrived, I felt extremely restless. I had to run away. Mom and Dad desperately attempted to prevent me from leaving the house completely undressed. In my deluded mind, I wanted to run to the park by the seashore and shed all my tears of regret. I wanted to cleanse myself of all my imperfect deeds. I wanted to begin my life all over as if I were an infant bursting into the world. After struggling and being restrained from leaving, I finally succumbed to my parents' strength and returned to my bedroom. Dad sat in a rocking chair in the dark corner of my room and guarded me until the morning. I'm sure he could hear my restless movements as I lay in the bed, far from slumber and unable to peacefully let go of the day.

I finally calmed down and fell into a partial sleep, and I experienced the sensation of leaving my body. My spirit looked down at my listless form. It wasn't time for me to leave the earth. Floating, I felt free and tempted to fly away from my scarred existence, but I couldn't abandon my parents. I wasn't ready to die. I decided I had a lot to live for, and this ounce of hope carried me forward. My spirit rejoined my body, and I slept.

During the winter of 1978–79, I slowly healed and returned to my ambitious self. Mom once again instilled a structured day. We worked together, creating collages out of cardboard cutouts. Working with my hands was therapeutic, and my convoluted thoughts subsided for the moment. I nestled myself on the couch in the den and listened to every classical record my parents owned. The sounds brought me bliss, helping me to cope with my plagued life. Still, I lagged behind my peers in my studies.

I returned to college for the 1979 spring semester. I enrolled in design studio and several other core courses, comprising ten credits instead of a full schedule of fifteen credits. I worked part-time for my father again, drafting roofing details. His office was located across Brooklyn, south of the college, which was about a thirty-minute drive.

My daily schedule consisted of attending classes in the morning and going to my part-time job in the afternoon. Dad's company was near the Atlantic Ocean, on an avenue that had few businesses lining the street: a corner pharmacy, a tire store, and a car dealership. His company was in a one-story building with a dim brick façade. I worked in the back at the end of a narrow hallway. The cramped space consisted of two drafting desks and big, flat drawers that stored documents for current projects.

A dull routine ensued, void of any inspiration, until I met Roger, a student in my design studio class, who just so happened to be the same man I'd previously admired from afar in the subway when I was living in the city and commuting to the Brooklyn campus. He was from the Middle East, and like me, pursuing a degree in architecture. He was polite and handsome, with thick, dark hair, dark eyes, pert lips, and a mustache. He seemed to be taken with me, always studying me carefully when we were together. After all, I always dressed beautifully and, with my dark features, I looked like his family.

Roger asked me to dinner, and I accepted. We drove through Manhattan late into the night. As I drove, he caressed my short, curly hair. I felt emotions I had never experienced with past boyfriends. I was attracted to Roger in every way, and the attraction was mutual. My heart and passion were on fire, and I became infatuated with Roger. I would do anything for the sake of his love.

Eventually, we became intimate, and I stayed the night at his apartment in the city. My work and studies were neglected as my intense romance with Roger ensued. Nothing else in the world mattered to me. It was Roger's world I obsessed about. We dined at fine restaurants, saw compelling movies, and enjoyed seeing *Carmen* at the Metropolitan Opera House. We shared similar values, and I was ready to marry Roger.

Although I was living at home during that time, I was careless about informing my parents of my whereabouts when I didn't return home after nights with Roger. I failed to formally introduce him to them, and they were hesitant in accepting my relationship with a man from the Middle East. Their subtle disapproval didn't hinder my blind love though.

Roger traveled home for the spring recess. After he returned, he was cool toward me, and any passion, affection, and infatuation he had for me ended abruptly. His father, a wealthy and devout Christian, disapproved of our relationship because I was Jewish. Our cultural heritage complicated our relationship as a couple.

Roger cared about his family, and he was torn. We got together often as our friendship grew, but there was no intimacy because of his strong connection to his family and their wishes. At the time, I couldn't comprehend the reasons for the change in our relationship. The further Roger drifted from me, the more I wanted his embrace.

I kept trying to garner his attention by dressing as elegantly as I could. I was convinced I could win him back, and he would defy his family for me. Deep down I knew I was fighting a lost cause, but I couldn't face the truth of our broken romance. I was despondent as Roger built an impenetrable wall around himself, and I was unrealistic in my persistence to break through.

Since many students commuted to the campus, the population never seemed bonded. They all had lives outside of the classroom, whether they worked part-time like me or were busy making other plans. I saw few opportunities to make friends. I depended on Roger's friendship outside of class. He kept telling me I would meet a nice Jewish man one day. I didn't believe him and thought it was a breakup line. I lost all hope of finding a soul mate, because I thought Roger was the one. In the crevices of my mind lurked the secrets of my episodic illness. I felt inadequate and insecure about my condition, and Roger's abstinence and cool behavior compounded my insecurities. I was certain that if he learned of my illness, he would avoid me altogether.

Dr. Samuels didn't realize how emotionally entwined I was in my unrequited relationship with Roger and that I couldn't move forward easily. The doctor always listened to me with a blank expression from his leather chair. He did not convey any practical caution or counsel on how to go on without Roger. Instead, he instructed me to avoid depending on my parents and to develop a support system elsewhere, which I found to be impossible. No one knew of my breakdowns, and I led a lonely life, concealing the truth from the few friends I had.

I was afraid if my peers learned of my illness, they would shun me and call me "the crazy woman."

CHAPTER 7

Between breakdowns—which at this point occurred every six months or so—I led a normal existence. I aspired to be popular, and I worked diligently at maintaining the conventions of daily life. Sessions with Dr. Samuels persisted with shallow words. We did not address the manifestations of my episodes. I carelessly denied my bleak periods between cycles. During my wellness, the doctor should have discussed the signs and symptoms and taught me how to avoid a potential meltdown. I desperately needed someone besides my parents to instill common sense into my complex existence because lurking in my subconscious was another developing break ready to surface.

Professor Tuttle, an instructor of design studio, announced a special two-week trip to Finland. I immediately, without hesitation, decided to participate in this journey to study architectural works by the world-renowned, Finnish architect, Alvar Aalto. He was known for designing natural biomorphic-shaped spaces and his creative application of building materials. His spaces were sensitive to the natural environs of evergreen trees and the multitude of curvy lakes in Finland.

Architects from all over the United States went on this excursion. We formed a group of about thirty people, enough to fill one tour bus. Finnish architecture students greeted our group when we landed in Helsinki. We toured the capital city for two days, then traveled north to visit Aalto's house and a factory where his curvilinear tables and chairs were manufactured. Aalto was creatively diverse in executing industrial design of furniture, blown glass vases, and buildings. Every design had curves showcasing his unique expression of form and function. He was a pioneer in individual expression during the first half of the twentieth century.

During our stay in Helsinki, I asked several male, Finnish students if there was a night spot we could go to. They told me about an old fortress on an island. I informed our American group. The Finnish students were shocked and disappointed when the entire tour group arrived for a tour of the island. They thought only females would show up and that they would all engage in sexual pleasure. The fortress was high up on the coast. It formed a silhouette against the dusky sky. All of us climbed to the fortress and looked out to the infinite sea. With such a sight before us and the cool breeze blowing, we were inspired to continue our tour of Finland to learn more about Alvar Aalto.

I befriended Ben, a middle-aged man who was a professor of architecture at a college in New York City. I was glib with him and crossed the boundary of becoming too familiar with a married man who was thirty years my senior. We connected on a personal level, creating a situation I did not plan for. A week went by, and we were on the second leg of our trip. Ben held my hand while exiting the bus. I was startled and tentative when he touched my hand. A devious student in my class snapped a photo of Ben and me from behind, capturing the fleeting, affectionate moment.

When we returned to the States, Professor Tuttle presented a slide show of our Finland trip for the school, and the photo of Ben and me holding hands was included in the presentation. That was an embarrassing moment for me. I could barely cope, since I was sensitive to the gossip and ridicule of the student body. My worst fears of being conspicuous surfaced. I felt like everyone's target.

While in Finland, I had called Jack, who was living in Belgium at the time. I relished the opportunity to speak with him and hear his familiar voice. I still thought of Jack two years after he had left me, even though my memory was fraught with abandonment. I was gravely disappointed but did not harbor any ill feelings toward him. He told me he would be traveling to New York the same time our group would be returning. I could barely contain my excitement.

When I arrived at the busy airport in New York, my father was patiently waiting for me. I suppose Dad was relieved to see me stable and not breaking down from the stresses of traveling with a group of strangers amid a hectic tour. I joyfully informed Dad that Jack would be arriving from Belgium at any moment. We waited and waited as I eagerly watched passengers descend and ascend the escalators. Jack never appeared, and Dad was sympathetic. I felt disappointed and depressed. Again, this cosmopolitan man had let me down. That was the end of my hope for reuniting with Jack.

Despite my disappointment and embarrassing moments, I was inspired by the works of Alvar Aalto. I felt motivated to succeed in design class and was determined to become a contextual designer like Aalto. The form of a structure was influenced by the environs. Seeing his works firsthand made it possible for me to move forward in my studies.

Following the trip to Finland, I enrolled in another design studio class Professor Tuttle taught in June 1979. The assignment reflected Aalto's natural architecture and entailed designing a space influenced by a score of music. I chose the symphonic sounds of "Prelude to the Afternoon of a Faun." by Claude Debussy to govern a sculptural space, just as the lakes and wooded areas influenced Aalto's designs years ago.

I purchased four sheets of plexiglass, each measuring ten-by-thirty inches. On each sheet, I used acrylic paint to depict colorful graphs that represented Debussy's musical passages, with symphonic crescendos painted in white. Each sheet was identical and looked like a cardiogram. I placed the sheets adjacent to each other, two inches apart. Together, the graphs formed spaces and rhythms of the musical score, its melodic composition, and the dynamic orchestration of sound. Looking at the space felt like being in a forest with leaping fawns as I navigated the paths illuminated by the glistening sun that filtered through the web of trees. Another student in the class copied my idea. I was annoyed and felt cheated out of my original idea, and to make matters worse, our professor never even addressed the issue. The summer course ended, and I passed it with flying colors. Professor Tuttle enjoyed my presentation as I played the recording of "Prelude to the Afternoon of a Faun."

During the remainder of the summer, I worked again at the hotel renovation site in New York City. This time I was responsible for managing the change orders over the initial budget of renovating the hotel. It was a desk job, and I had spare time, so I studied my textbook of construction practices.

A tall, rotund man, Arty, was the chief consultant. He was employed by the general contractor, as I was, and he came by my desk and spoke to me in a humorous, robust manner.

"Bubbala, you are on a construction site. Get rid of the textbook."

Arty was a jovial, boisterous genius who had created several patents for curtain wall designs. I closed the book until he left the office and then continued studying.

❋

Several coworkers suggested I pursue my current job full-time in lieu of completing architecture school. It was tempting to continue my career in construction, but I had to complete my professional degree.

More employees worked in the construction office than had during the previous summer. A tough woman named Harriet was one of the project managers. She coordinated the subcontractors' documents and supervised the construction workers during the final phase of the process.

Harriet cursed profusely as an attempt to demonstrate authority among a sea of male construction workers. We were the only females employed by the general contractor, and it was difficult to command respect in a male-dominated environment. My father, who was one of the subcontractors, had worked with Harriet, so she was interested in befriending me. I was surprised by her efforts since she was my superior. My job entailed minimal effort compared to Harriet's job, which was enormously demanding. We remained friends and had lunch together numerous times over the years. Harriet never knew of my illness, which remained an incessant burden for me to carry. I always cherished her friendship, and she continued to be my link to the construction world. She was focused and successful in a man's world and eventually landed a prominent position with a real estate developer. I was honored to be her friend.

CHAPTER 8

The summer of 1979 went by with uncanny speed, and on Labor Day, September 2, my parents and I moved to our dream house on the coast of Long Island Sound. It was in the same neighborhood as our old house. The backyard featured two tiers of land rolling down to a cliff high above the seashore. It was simply paradise.

I became nostalgic leaving the house I grew up in. All of the memories of my youth surfaced, and it was time to let go and begin again. I also experienced a powerful emptiness as I yearned for Roger, even though he chose his family over me. I knew he would admire our new home and perhaps be attracted to me once more. I pined for his touch, and I was on a lonely crusade, mourning my past illusions of Roger. In his absence I obsessed about him. He was moving on with his life, and I was stuck being governed by my lurking illness.

Dad hired me to renovate the kitchen in our new home. The kitchen had a panoramic view of the Long Island Sound. The view was inspiring, and I took pleasure in designing the kitchen and extending the dining room with practical form and beauty. I chose cherrywood cabinets, which were classic enough to endure the passage of time. I filled the wall in the back of the galley kitchen with cabinets from floor to ceiling, much like Alvar Aalto's kitchen. I also designed a wooden deck with stairs that led to the garden, where we could spend hours soaking up the heavenly beauty and aura of the seacoast.

I installed my drafting desk in a room that was originally the den. Fortunately, the desk didn't face the coastal view, as it would have distracted me from my work. The house was peaceful, with more living space than our previous home. Mom decorated the house in an eclectic contemporary style, including tan couches, purple shag rugs, and contemporary artwork. She demonstrated originality in her interior design.

Midway into the fall semester, I suffered from a mini-breakdown, although I struggled to hold myself together. I imagined people were conspiring against me and that I was extremely alone, an outcast. The stress of moving to a new home and being embarrassed by Professor Tuttle's second slideshow, which featured a picture of Ben and me holding hands, weighed heavily on my conscience. I imagined everyone could see my truth, my inadequacy, my inferiority, my "looseness." It was impossible to return to school where everyone was laughing at me and snickering about my promiscuity. I had to withdraw from the fall semester at the Brooklyn college, which set me back once again from reaching the finish line.

Designing the kitchen and dining room for our new house kept me busy during this crisis. I spent time by traveling to tile stores, kitchen cabinet stores, and plumbing supply stores and sorted out the details of the new kitchen.

One day, my mother and I were sitting in the kitchen when the community synagogue called. They informed Mom of the most disturbing news. Todd had died. He had gotten tangled in an operating drill. I burst into tears and shook. Grief enveloped me as I recalled the memory of asking Todd to marry me and move to California. I visited his home while his parents were sitting Shiva and expressed my condolences as best I could. I caught a glimpse of Todd's grieving grandparents, who acknowledged me with recognition. I was the nice Jewish girl around the corner who once dated Todd and could have been included in his future.

When the spring semester arrived, I returned to school while holding onto the precious memory of Todd. Mourning him outweighed my embarrassment from Professor Tuttle's slideshow. Construction commenced on our house, and my design for the kitchen and dining room began to come alive.

I enrolled in an American government course taught by Professor Edwards. She was a feminist who didn't wear any makeup and sported fashionably masculine, dark, thick-framed glasses. She firmly believed that women should have equal opportunity in the workforce and be compensated as much as their male counterparts.

Professor Edwards created a mock primary election that the class would participate in. The class was divided into two groups, and each group chose a student to campaign for presidency. My team chose me, and I had to write a speech that addressed the economy and how I would improve it if elected president. I struggled to write a compelling speech, so my father helped me. My speech won, and while I felt deeply honored, I also felt awkward since it was really my father's influence that brought about my success. Following the mock election, Professor Edwards showered me with attention—often conversing about the politics of the day. Although I found her strong feminist outlook intimidating, in her class, I learned how politics can determine and influence human existence. Despite the sloppy architecture and the campus's need for renovation, I appreciated attending the school because I had a lot to learn from the diligent professors who taught their subjects with the same enthusiasm as Professor Edwards did.

My infatuation with Roger diminished with time. As the months passed, my grief at the loss of Todd faded as well. I was determined and ready to move on with finding Mr. Right. In the spring, I participated in a Jewish singles event where I met Ron. He was my age, yet I was cautious. I feared that Ron, a seemingly typical person, would learn about my psychotic side and reject me.

Ron was an artist who earned a bachelor of fine arts degree from a college in Boston. He was too conventional and lacked the imagination to be a stellar artist, but he was confident in his abilities to depict reality. He painted teacups and chairs on canvas. He did not possess my wild, unchanneled imagination.

Ron was impressed with my vocation as an architect. I was attracted to his beautiful, blue-green eyes and masculine hands. As our friendship developed, Ron showed me his studio in the basement of his family's suburban, split-level house. A painting of luminous yellow teacups rested on his easel. They were magically realistic. Then I noticed all of his practice paintings leaning against the wall. He executed the painting over and over until he achieved a hyperreal rendition of the teacups.

I met Ron's mother and two of his sisters, who were gathered in the kitchen. My hasty impression of his family was they hadn't suffered my mental handicaps and were stable, even-tempered, and shallow. It was clear, based on her questions, that Ron's mother recognized my artistic bent; she had learned I was an architecture student, and she seemed to be impressed and quietly content with her son's choice of women. I suppose she surmised that Ron and I would complement each other and share common experiences.

Ron's sisters hardly acknowledged me as they continued their conversation with each other. I stood awkwardly until Ron took me to the den to meet his father. Ron was hesitant about introducing me to his father, and I did not experience a warm welcome. Instead, I perceived a cold recognition brimming with judgment. I felt his father could see through me to the perils of my past. I believed his father thought I was not good enough for his son, upon whom he had a strong hold. According to Ron, his father constantly demanded he paint the teacups over and over until the depiction was perfect, and developing an imagination was prohibitive. Over time, Ron allowed his father's attitude to impact how he felt about me. Ron became subtly critical of me.

This artistic man had a strong connection to his neighborhood temple, and his faith was even more fervent than his family's. He became extremely pious and eventually separated himself from my secular ways of life. We were never intimate since he observed the orthodox creed about sex being appropriate only in the context of marriage. Eventually, Ron joined the orthodox community and abandoned me. He believed I was not pure enough for him to marry. I felt like I was on the outside and believed I wasn't good enough because I took his underlying criticisms personally, not realizing I did not have to abide by his views.

Before the strictly conservative version of Ron emerged, he took me to an exhibit of David Hockney's paintings. The artist was there to meet his jubilant fans. Ron eagerly sought Mr. Hockney's autograph as I stood on the sidelines, entirely disinterested in meeting this famous artist who was generous with his salutations and signature. At the time, I wasn't passionate about the field of art, and I didn't think obtaining an autograph from Mr. Hockney was important. Ron had difficulty accepting my lack of enthusiasm for his idol in realism. I hadn't heard of Mr. Hockney until we attended the exhibit. Much later in life, I appreciated Hockney's work and style. He had a long resume of painting and photography. Figurative realism comprised Hockney's earliest period. The colors in Ron's teacup paintings were reminiscent of Hockney's colorful work. Ron's teacups were velvet and fluid compared to Hockney's bold, graphic style. Hockney painted his colors graphically flat, yet they had a depth and perspective that defined a distinctive style.

Since I wasn't interested in Mr. Hockney's autograph, Ron felt I didn't fit his life. Ron was an uneventful artist, and it was absurd that I continued my relationship with him. I withstood his authoritative father and his critical nature toward me. I was needy and afraid of being alone, suffering from a deep-seated feeling of inadequacy, so I settled for a man who did not respect me.

CHAPTER 9

At the end of spring semester in 1980, Columbia University offered a special urban design and planning course in Paris. It was a six-week course during May and June, a lovely time to be in France. I embraced this opportunity, leaving Ron behind while still searching for Mr. Right amid my exploration of a romantic city. I put all of my perils aside, denying any possibility of a breakdown. In the moment, I felt steady, as if I had never broken down, and my yearning for adventure and search for a mate were compelling.

I boarded the plane to France in the middle of May without any plans for where I would live during the next six weeks. I don't remember if my parents or Dr. Samuels were aware of this. I befriended a Parisian father and daughter on the plane who were on their way home. We shared a taxi after we landed. They guided me to the college office and education facility in Montmartre, an old, artistic section of Paris. I arrived just in time to arrange an apartment rental and met a student who was in the same predicament as me. Bob was tall and lanky and had sparkling brown eyes. He was neat and put-together—he looked like an architect—and, sure enough, he was studying architecture at a college in New Jersey. He was attending the urban design course as well. We became friends instantly, and my loneliness abated after this meeting.

Fate was kind to me. My apartment wouldn't be ready for three days, so I rented a room in a small inn about a half mile from the school. The inn was a strange place: all the guests showered in a private stall on the ground floor adjacent to the kitchen, and the toilet was tucked in a little closet off the staircase landing.

A light breakfast of coffee and a pastry was included in the rent for my tiny room. I was alone in the room with a small bed and chest of drawers, but I didn't mind. This was an adventure in the making.

The school quarters consisted of a two-story structure with an interior courtyard surrounded by classrooms. It was an elegant space. Students gathered in the courtyard before and after their classes. Aside from the urban planning course, a program in fashion design also was available under the auspices of a New York fashion school.

Besides Bob, I became familiar with Debbie and Frances, who were enrolled in the fashion program. Debbie was quiet, rotund, serious, and smoked cigarettes. Frances had dark, curly hair and olive skin. She was painfully skinny and smoked cigarettes to maintain her delicate figure.

Luckily, the coursework in the urban program was not challenging. It required touring an array of buildings and urban sites in Paris and evaluating the architectural influence of Napoleon's rule: the uniform façades of low-story buildings and the vistas and monuments created from widened streets forming axes. Everyone took numerous photographs to create a pictorial presentation that would accompany an oral discourse on the relevance of city planning amid the influence of Baron Haussmann, who improved the living quarters and general appearance of the old city, Paris, in 1870.

The assistant professor, Mary, was dedicated and worked closely with us as we prepared our presentations. She assisted Professor Williams, who taught this special course for years. They maintained vast knowledge of urban history and the development of Paris. I didn't pay close attention to their lectures because I was distracted by the romantic historical aura of the city. Even though Roger faded from my memory, I longed to walk the streets and share the beauty of Paris with him. That didn't last, though, as I became familiar with the students in the program. A handsome man named William was enrolled in the urban course. He was tall and had electric blue eyes and tanned skin. He lived in Connecticut and told me he was an excellent sailor who often sailed the Long Island Sound. I felt a connection with William since we were both so far from the familiar waters of the Long Island Sound. William was soft-spoken and kept to himself. He remained a mystery to me because he was a very private person.

I also met Doug, who was in his last semester of architecture school at Columbia University. He was my height with thick, black hair and a scholarly appearance.

I was instantly drawn to him, but he was taken. His girlfriend was enrolled in another program in Paris. She was petite, spoke fluent French, and was animated. She was bored with Doug and enthralled by William. This was an aggravating love triangle, because I would have forgotten everyone I ever dated just to be with Doug.

Despite my strong desire to be with Doug, I continued to explore Paris with Bob. We had grown close and were comfortable with each other. I established a supportive relationship in a foreign land with Bob even though I pined for Doug.

Bob rented an apartment a mile or two away from the place I inhabited in the Eiffel Tower district. My room, which had a connecting bathroom, was part of a larger apartment. An older Lebanese woman and her thirty-year-old son also lived in the slightly gloomy and traditionally decorated apartment. She often invited me to spend time with her in the tiny kitchen while she baked the most delicious fruit tarts. She kept a collection of paintings in the pantry created by her deceased husband, whom she had loved and cherished. She was small, frail, and talkative in English. She whispered in my ear that if only I were Catholic, I would be suitable for her son. I was startled but flattered that she approved of me. She inquired if I knew anyone who could rent the apartment below, and I thought of Debbie from the fashion program. The apartment was fully furnished, and the owners were on vacation in southern Europe. Debbie happily rented the apartment, and she thanked me heartily.

The apartment Debbie rented included a dining room furnished with a long dining table. She invited me to use the table surface to work on my project for the urban design course. Instead of toiling on the assignment to create a photo presentation of Paris and prepare for the discourse about Haussmann's influence on the old city, I chose to study an apartment building that had an interior atrium with a pool on the ground floor. Henri Sauvage designed it in the mid-twentieth century. Sauvage piqued my curiosity and sparked my attention with his novel design that integrated private and public spaces. I was able to retrieve the building documents, consisting of floor plans and elevations, from the Parisian building department. I put the drawings, which were executed on a large scale, on the dining room table. I diligently scaled down the floor plans, although it was tedious to transfer the drawings accurately into plans that would fit on a notebook page. I color-coded the plans to distinguish public spaces from private ones.

Bob and I walked all over Paris and rendered scenes of old buildings by the Seine. Bob sketched much faster than me. He quickly drew the entire composition then developed the details such as the façade materials, the windows, roof, and surrounding context. Meanwhile, I began rendering the details such as the windows and a section of the façade, building the entire scene sections at a time. Bob was a stellar student who learned about illustration in accordance with the conventions of the practice of architecture. He never deviated from the norm.

One day, Bob invited me to his apartment. It was a charming space filled with light. He prepared a simple meal of sautéed zucchini. That was my first time eating this vegetable, and it was delicious. I appreciated his efforts and his stable company. Our friendship endured the entire time in Paris. Our relationship was purely platonic and stifled from developing into a romance because I always had my sight on unattainable men.

Every day, I walked to class in Montmartre. It was a forty-five-minute jaunt, and on the way, I stopped at an outdoor café to have a café au lait and delicious croissant. This solitary, daily routine filled me with joy. After I arrived at school, I walked the streets with the class, taking photos with an expensive Nikon camera. I inched my way toward Doug, hoping he would notice me. He didn't. He was traveling with his own agenda, and I believe he was discontent about not knowing what would follow his last semester at college. He would have been content as a perpetual student. I didn't think about Jack, Ron, or Roger because I was preoccupied with my fantasy about Doug. To have a conversation with him was challenging and awkward, as my infatuation with him got in the way. I finally remarked to him that he must feel excited to finally complete the endless architecture program. He snapped at me, blurting out that he was unable to find a job. I was so drawn to him that I ignored his angry response.

On my own time, I visited art museums, including the Louvre, and viewed paintings from the Renaissance to contemporary times. Paris was the home of impressionists, and I felt a strong connection to many of the artists' works. At the time, art was not my passion, despite my intense appreciation.

One evening, William, Doug, his girlfriend, and I met for dinner. We were cordial to one another, and Doug's girlfriend couldn't disguise her attraction to William. The conversation was trivial and awkward. Doug was cold and evasive, and William was soft-spoken. When we finally left the bistro, Doug's girlfriend walked ahead with William, while Doug and I trudged behind. Doug seemed desperate for conversation and criticized the way I dressed, especially my top. My T-shirt was black with long sleeves, featuring an appliqué of flowered patterns around my chest area. He rudely remarked that a Parisian woman would never wear that. I was stunned and at a loss for words. Despite his crass comments, I foolishly remained attracted to him. The more anguish I felt, the harder I tried to garner his approval, but nothing ever blossomed.

My trip to Paris was near its end when I traveled to Cannes, in the south of France, with the two students from the fashion program. Debbie, Frances, and I took the train from Paris and enjoyed seeing the gorgeous French countryside. We were weekend vagabonds seeking thrills amid the bustling Riviera. After we arrived, we discovered a small hotel across from the train station, which we immediately settled into. One of my first activities was immersing myself in a warm bath while Debbie and Frances smoked their cigarettes. I felt like an outsider since I didn't smoke, but I pushed those thoughts aside. I was eager to absorb the sights and sounds of Cannes.

I walked alone around the slightly neglected and worn, old city. However, the shops were lovely, and the household items were attractively displayed and expensive. I managed to communicate in my rusty French because the merchants preferred to speak in their native tongue. I was searching for a gift for my Lebanese landlord. I could afford only a signature jar of rose jam. When I presented this aromatic gift, she seemed extremely disappointed. She probably expected a vase or tablecloth rather than an edible item.

My friends and I spent a glorious day on the vast Mediterranean beach. Debbie and Frances lounged on their stomachs on beach chairs. They sunned themselves with their bathing suit tops unstrapped so as not to create tan lines. They frequently smoked, so I strolled down the beach, passing many topless women. One woman, who had a scarred breast, was probably a survivor of breast cancer, but that did not deter her from enjoying the freedom of being topless. I stood out on the crowded beach because I wore a red, one-piece bathing suit that enhanced my figure and created mystery about my nudity. I finally reached the shoreline and immersed myself in the cool water, recollecting days I spent on the beach in my youth. I swam out to a large float brimming with people resting and tanning under the beaming sun. I climbed aboard and briefly joined the wet, toned bodies before returning to the stale company of the chain smokers.

Exhausted from the sea and glaring sun, we moved in slow motion back to the small hotel. We decided to embrace the experience of the Riviera to the fullest, so we took a train to Monte Carlo that evening. The vistas from the train's curvy track looked magnificent and featured cliffsides overlooking the Mediterranean Sea.

I wore a striped cotton dress that elongated my tall figure, and my short hair was curly from swimming in the salty water. Debbie wore a conservative, black dress. Frances wore a ballerina-like dress with cowboy boots. The three of us marched to our own beats: the tall one, the rotund one, and the skinny one.

We arrived in Monaco after several hours on the train. We ducked into a casino but quickly exited when we realized gambling was too expensive for us. The casino, like all of Monaco, was elegantly furnished and served the wealthiest clients in Europe. We walked a short distance and stopped at a tavern. We had a drink, and Debbie suddenly fainted. Shocked, Frances and I stood over her. Debbie revived quickly, and we did not question the cause of her lapse. Then we descended a hill and walked to a famous disco. As we approached the entrance, two men from Italy engaged us in conversation. They seemed to be infatuated with Frances, who looked somewhat Italian. They ignored Debbie and me, which made me feel unattractive.

Frances gloated and remained with the two strangers all evening and into the early morning. Debbie and I danced for a while and then sat in a booth, nursing our drinks. A man sitting at a table close to the entrance, a small distance from where we sat, called out to me. He was drunk and looked like Robert Redford dressed in a white suit. I ignored his bellowing until he stumbled over to our booth and stood before me. He must have seen an angry young woman because he backed off. I was concerned with how we were going to get back to our hotel, so I was surprised when the two men Frances befriended took us back to Cannes in their Volkswagen. The two-hour ride seemed longer because I was impatient to return. Even though the men were kind to ensure our safety, I was finished with them and the whole situation. We rested and then took the train back to Paris. Frances and Debbie sat in the smoking car. I ventured to a nonsmoking car so I could enjoy the clean air and relaxation. I was alone again.

CHAPTER 10

It was my last week in Paris. I was extremely anxious about presenting my project to the class, and I downed a glass of wine beforehand to soothe my nerves. I slowly tacked my petite drawings to the wall as I glanced at the attentive group of students and professors. I spoke of Sauvage's design: a unique building with four floors of apartments encircling a ground-floor atrium, which housed a pool open to both tenants and the public. The entire apartment complex centered around the pool, which was a new concept when it was built in the 1920s, half a century after Haussmann's "rebuilding Paris." The relationship of private and public space in Sauvage's apartment building echoed the redesign of Haussmann's Paris, where rows of private townhouses formed parks and vistas of public spaces and monuments.

Mary, the assistant professor, blatantly remarked that the subject I chose to study was tangential to the course assignment. She and Professor Williams, however, said they still enjoyed my presentation of colorful floor plans depicting the analysis of public and private space integral in Sauvage's design. Bob presented an excellent photographic journey of Haussmann's Paris. Since he and the rest of the students did not deviate from the assignment, they each received a perfect grade. My presentation, although excellent in providing an analysis of public and private space, received an "above average" grade.

At an end-of-session party at the school building, I stood idly near the buffet table when a group of visiting French students attempted to engage me. They probably thought I was Parisian, with my short, curly hairstyle and slim dress that hugged my figure. I saw that Doug, who was standing nearby with his girlfriend and William, was watching the Parisian men surrounding me. I pushed my way through the dense crowd and headed toward him. We almost spoke to each other, but an aggressive Parisian architecture student intercepted my attention. We conversed and exchanged phone numbers. His name was Pascal. He was gregarious and good-looking, with vivid blue eyes and cropped, black hair. Still, my thoughts lingered on Doug, who was in his own world. I greeted Bob as I drifted away from Doug, although I couldn't break away from Doug's indifference toward me. That preoccupation kept me from appreciating Bob's company.

After the party and on my final night in Paris, Bob escorted me back to my apartment. We were idly passing time in my room when Pascal called and invited me to a disco with his French friends. I accepted Pascal's invitation and was remiss in not inviting Bob to join us. I was rude and didn't consider his feelings. We said goodbye. There was no embrace or kiss and no sign of regret. He told me he was traveling to England to see his "honey." I was surprised to learn, after all our time together, he had a girlfriend. I suddenly felt as though I wasn't good enough to be his girlfriend. Maybe he fabricated the girlfriend to get back at me for abandoning him for Pascal.

I never saw Bob again. I did not miss him or think about him since he ended our friendship in an uncaring manner. His girlfriend, if she existed, probably attended the same Ivy League college he did. In our last moment together, I gave Bob a roll of film for his camera since I had plenty. We parted knowing it was the end of a needed friendship and a bond too weak to endure the distance.

I took a cab to Pascal's apartment and met him in the alcove. He didn't invite me into his apartment. Perhaps he was embarrassed to reveal he lived with his parents. I learned that his father was a prominent psychiatrist in Paris, which spurred thoughts of my recent perils that were hidden from everyone. We waited for a long time until his friends showed up. Then we made our way to the disco. Pascal wore electric blue pants and a matching jacket. I wore a yellow-and-purple-striped clingy dress and a lavender blazer. I looked Parisian but couldn't join in the conversation, as Pascal's friends spoke French the entire time. This exclusion lasted the whole evening, and Pascal, who tried his best to converse with me, expressed how he was ashamed of their rude behavior.

The disco was dark and crowded with people. I found it difficult to stay close to Pascal, and time lagged. I was bored with the flamboyant scene of the disco. I felt alienated from Pascal's friends and had to keep demanding that Pascal's friend return my blazer, which he borrowed to gain entrance to the disco. It was an intolerable outing.

After visiting the disco, we ambled the streets of Paris until we stopped at an ice cream parlor. We were famished. Pascal's friends continued ignoring me, and I finally got so angry that I got up from the table, leaving my ice cream, and left without saying goodbye. Pascal immediately followed me. He said he felt terrible about the night turning into a catastrophe for me. He hailed a cab, and I returned to my apartment.

I went home the following day feeling satisfied overall with my trip to Paris and relieved that I survived the stresses of the trip. My father met me at the airport and took me home. I was eager to tell my parents about my experience in France. I had purchased a small gift for my mother, Parisian soap, and I regretted not giving her perfume instead. I bought larger items for myself: a pink-and-black button-down blouse and a champagne-colored pinstripe suit, which were discounted at Printemps, a Parisian department store in the heart of Paris. The store's tremendous atrium exhibited clothing displays from different designers that were organized as separate boutiques surrounding the central, open space. Since I was thin, I was able to wear a large array of clothing, which made choosing outfits difficult.

I returned to the same old grind of seeing Dr. Samuels twice a week. We talked about my experiences in Paris, and the doctor attributed my stability to my time living with the Lebanese woman. He explained that I had successfully maintained a support system other than my parents; therefore, I was able to cope with difficult social situations. I was able to endure my feelings of isolation and loneliness, whether real or imagined, that I internalized and carried everywhere. Reflecting on my stable success, Dr. Samuels continually encouraged me to develop a support network with strangers instead of my parents. The doctor never convened with my parents to discuss a game plan for addressing the symptoms of my cyclic illness. He mistakenly believed I had separation issues and anxiety that stemmed from my mother, whom he viewed as unsympathetic in providing emotional support. According to Dr. Samuels, I was successful in Paris with a group of strangers; therefore, I could be successful in New York.

I struggled in my shallow attempts to survive the tribulations of living in New York even though I was living at home. I felt alone and disconnected. Instead of forming a team with my parents, Dr. Samuels created a schism between us that only made things worse. Fears of a lonely future prevailed, and I struggled to keep my thoughts from falling into a pattern of darkness.

CHAPTER 11

Ron, the pious artist, was back in my life. Memories of my times with Doug and Bob faded, and I couldn't tolerate being alone without a man in my life. Our relationship remained superficial, as Ron became steadily more religious, and his subtle, underlying criticism of my lifestyle prevailed. I was not a pious woman hiding behind the veils of orthodox religious traditions.

In the summer of 1980, Ron and I went swimming in the Long Island Sound. The water was cool and refreshing in the heat of August. We were alone in the calm waters, so I slid my bikini top off, exposing my breasts to Ron. I felt liberated to swim topless. Ron was shocked and reprimanded me for the unlawful act of swimming topless at a public beach where anyone could show up at any time. He was extremely embarrassed and demanded I put my top back on. At the time, I denied how prudent Ron was, and his startling reaction resonated in my thoughts—I was impure and not good enough for his affections. I was simply emulating my experience at the Riviera, where all the women were topless, and I wondered how Ron would tolerate their culture. He dwelled in his pious world, far from appreciation of my womanhood, building a wall between us that was impossible to break through. Yet I continued dating Ron. I was too passive to let go of him, but we had very little in common, and I didn't anticipate his break from the secular world was on the horizon.

Later in August, Ron invited me to partake in a five-day program in upstate New York sponsored by a Jewish college youth group. I innocently responded that I would be delighted to participate in this summer journey. After all, Paris had been an adventure, and I coped with the stresses of that trip. I believed I was stronger than ever. I was invincible and could brave new experiences.

Ron and I drove in my little, yellow car. We took the New York State Thruway north and then veered west on a narrow route through the countryside. The memory of my breakdown on this same road haunted me as a heavy secret I kept from Ron. I feared the truth of my breakdown would be exposed, and I suffered immense embarrassment. I knew Ron could never understand or accept me, and the success of surviving my trip to Paris was fading. When we arrived, I was impressed with the grounds but concerned the camp was in the middle of nowhere. I felt trapped with no means to escape, and camp policy prohibited anyone from leaving the campus during the five-day program. That was the first rule.

I parted from Ron after we checked in and then carried my luggage to an assigned bunk on the periphery of the grounds. The girls' bunks were separated from the boys'.

Two girls in my bunk already knew each other. Unlike me, they were active in the Jewish youth group. They had brown hair, brown eyes, and well-endowed bodies. They said I was lucky to have a boyfriend. I felt their envy.

The program was organized into separate activities, and the camp population was divided into groups. Each camper could choose two activities daily, such as Israeli dancing, a discussion group about Jewish authors or the Torah, and how biblical stories related to current affairs.

Ron and I participated in different groups. He became buddies with the two girls from my bunk, and his behavior toward me became complacent since I was different from the Jewish girls at camp. I dressed with an artistic flare that stood out in the crowd.

I felt Ron's disapproval as he was influenced by the domineering girl and her pious friend. They formed a clique and purposely excluded me, and Ron was swept away by their Jewish identity.

Since we were forbidden to leave the grounds, I felt trapped. I had no way to escape my perceptions of growing hostility around me. I participated in a morning discussion group and voiced my opinion about current affairs and the complicated existence of Israel. It was important to me that I be heard, acknowledged, and respected. I grasped the opportunity to shine, which I achieved for a fleeting moment until a male camper, who sat across from me, told me to shut up. Did I offend him? Was I being too negative about the state of Israel? I was startled and floundered for a retort, but I remained silent and embarrassed.

I felt as though everyone was looking at me like I was different. I felt like I didn't belong. A wave of paranoia was slowly enveloping me, sweeping me away into a surreal time warp. I felt isolated and alienated from the campers and humanity at large.

Somehow, I made it to the next morning discussion group. Rabbi Hubman led the small group. He was the director of a Jewish youth group at a college in Brooklyn. He eagerly greeted me and said that I must be very knowledgeable of the Kabbalah, Jewish mysticism, and the creation of man in God's path. I was skeptical of his inappropriate, friendly overture, and I didn't understand what he meant by the Kabbalah. I was too jarred by the male camper who had told me to shut up in the previous discussion group.

A petite female camper shunned me because, it seemed, she was jealous of the attention the rabbi gave me. She was hostile to me throughout the five-day program. Rabbi Hubman didn't realize he should have praised all the campers. Despite his awkward flattery, I began to imagine everyone was conspiring against me, a familiar, gnawing feeling. I fell short of my unrealistic expectation that everyone should admire and like me. I started to unravel. My demons were surfacing, and I felt like I was in enemy territory.

During lunch in the dining hall, all of the campers stood up and formed a line. Rabbi Hubman led the line as we danced around the hall. I was behind the rabbi. He purposely strayed away from the line, leaving me to lead the joyous group. The petite girl was behind me. I led the line to the exit, but no one followed. Instead, they kept dancing around the dining hall and following the petite girl. Why did Rabbi Hubman keep making me the center of activities? I guess he thought I was artistic and more spiritual than most of his students. Around the second or third day, I stopped participating in activities and hid in my bunk.

Shabbat arrived, and I reluctantly attended the religious service on Friday night. The entire group of campers gathered in a circle around the rabbi under a large tent. Two female campers and the rabbi chose me to go to the center and light the Shabbat candles. I was surprised and anxious to perform this ritual. I felt like I was conspicuous and the target of ridicule. As I lit the candles, everyone recited a prayer to welcome the spirit of Shabbat, the seventh day of rest and reflection. I made the motions, but my mind and spirit were somewhere else. I continued to think all the campers harbored hostility toward me. Ron had left me to fend for myself since he fell under the spell of the two strong-willed girls in my bunk.

The night was cool, and the sky was clear and full of stars. I decided to take a stroll and venture outside the boundary of the campus. I felt free from my prison for a moment, but then a camp patrolman found me and forced me to board a bus and return to the grounds. I was furious and felt violated. Ron must have informed the patrol I was missing. I desperately wanted to abandon the program, but I was forced to stay. I caved in to my situation as I returned to the bunk, succumbing to the authority of the smothering patrol officer who kept me as a prisoner. I climbed to the top bunk bed and lay flat on the hard mattress, staring at the ceiling.

I endured my crippling fears by holding my Bible close to my heart and praying God would bring me peace in such a painful situation. I attempted to sleep, but the rapid beating of my heart and racing thoughts kept me awake. I berated myself for past failures, imagined and real. The two strong-willed girls returned to the bunk and noticed me lying still on my bed. I'm sure they sensed I was struggling psychologically. One girl blurted out that she knew of a husband who had agreed to have his troubled wife lobotomized. She hit a nerve and compounded my fears of being locked away and forgotten. I became paralyzed with fear.

Lurking in the back of my mind was a memory of being an assistant counselor at a Jewish camp in the Berkshires the August before my sophomore year in college. I had taken over for the assistant who left at the end of July. My responsibility involved looking after twelve-year-old campers. After a few days, the group of twelve campers had turned on me and called me a witch. They continually taunted me, mostly because I had recited the Hebrew prayers at Shabbat service poorly. The counselor I assisted couldn't control the mean-spirited girls. Soon after, when all were at activities, I packed my duffle bag and abandoned an unforgiving situation.

The two girls avoided me as I lay frozen in my bunk bed until the end of the program, enduring a few days without sleep and food. Ron enjoyed himself and neglected me as I was melting down. We left on a hot day in August. Ron said goodbye to his clique of headstrong, devious girls, and they exchanged contact information.

CHAPTER 12

Ron finished his farewells as I stood idle and impatient, feeling foolish and dejected. Finally, we walked across the campus to the parking lot. It felt like a century had passed since our arrival, and I was extremely relieved to leave this prison. Ron had good experiences making new friends, so he couldn't fathom what was crippling me. I expressed my outrage over the camp patrol forcing me back onto the campus when I innocently strolled outside the grounds. It occurred to me Ron probably didn't care what happened to me during the program, since he was under the spell of the girls from my bunk. They were extremely active in the Jewish community, and I wasn't. I did not live up to Ron's standards of being Jewish. I believed those backstabbers convinced Ron I was loose, promiscuous, and unacceptable by his religious standards.

Since I was driving us home, I managed to hold myself together. I continued to imagine I was a pariah, and everyone was conspiring against me. I was an outcast struggling in my isolation, and my feelings of inadequacy were immense. Ron was angry with me for expressing that I found the enclave unbearable.

I hadn't slept for days, and I was breaking down while on autopilot. Ron didn't realize I wasn't well. He had no experience with mental health issues, so he didn't know what a breakdown looked like. We finally reached his house, and I said goodbye, not knowing if I would ever see him again. When I arrived home, my parents immediately knew I was not well by my straggly appearance and distant, stone-like glare. I brought the fears and isolation from camp home with me, and I imagined my parents were planning to send me away and lock me up in a hospital forever. I was barren of any hope and deep in despair with gripping paranoia.

Pushing my mom and dad aside, I went to my bedroom and placed my bags on the bed. I closed the door behind me and ignored my panic-stricken parents. I began to pace back and forth anxiously and plan my escape. I could leave through the front door, but my parents would try to stop me. I had to break away before they imprisoned me.

The 1975 movie *One Flew Over the Cuckoo's Nest* was about a male patient dwelling in a psych ward who was eventually given a lobotomy because his raucous, rebellious behavior was influencing other patients in the ward. This story haunted me. I was extremely paranoid that my parents would corner me and order the doctor to perform a lobotomy to control my breakdowns. They were afraid I would end up dead. My paranoia kept me from realizing that lobotomies weren't performed any longer. Fifty thousand lobotomies were enacted before the medical community deemed the procedure too extreme. Scientists were developing new psychotropic medicines to address mental illness. Putting reality aside, the imagery of *One Flew Over the Cuckoo's Nest* was devastating. I was desperate to run away from my distraught world, a limbo in anguish where I was trapped in a web of imagined ill-fates.

I escaped through the window in the bathroom. Haunted by my imagination, I believed I was escaping from carnage, martyrdom, isolation, alienation, and the unforgiving civil war between the socialists and capitalists. It was hot outside but I didn't feel the oppressive heat as I walked with manic energy. I decided to walk to California, the Golden State, where I had wanted to go with Todd, my friend who had died. I could start a new life in California. I walked and walked. Heavy rains began to fall, and I took shelter in a small hut I discovered in someone's backyard.

Meanwhile, my parents filed a missing person's report and asked the county police to find me. Officers eventually found me walking after the rain ceased. I managed to remain dry in the little hut during the heavy downpour, but I had walked more than six miles when the police found me. They took me to the county hospital's emergency room.

I stubbornly refused to reveal my identity, and eventually the police summoned my desperate parents to come to the hospital and confirm who I was. My father left my mother at home and arrived to the hospital. Dad, fraught with the fear and anxiety of losing his daughter, braved the circumstances and always confronted big obstacles in his attempts to watch over me. My breaks were beyond his control, but he never gave up on me.

I did not see my father when he arrived at the emergency room, and I did not ask to see him. I was allowed to make a phone call, and I called Ron's house since I had memorized his phone number. His father answered the phone and was cold to me. His low opinion of me was obvious. I hung up the phone feeling more isolated.

As I was escorted to the desk where my information was processed, I passed a cubicle with a slightly open curtain, and I could see an injured young woman screaming in pain. Her boyfriend had cut her from head to toe, and the shock of witnessing her bloody body affected me. The scene briefly brought me out of my anxious spiral.

The nurse at the desk searched for an available bed in the psych ward where I could spend the night. She offered me a cup of orange juice, which I gratefully accepted since I had not eaten or slept for days. I was a victim of my mind, fighting an internal war and seeking solace from my endless battle. I was a prisoner of my delusional world. I asked the nurse if I could have a cup of milk. I drained it quickly. I could have drunk a gallon of milk, but the nurse limited me to one cup.

Late in the evening, a nurse escorted me to the second-floor, locked psych unit. The institutional ward with yellow walls was worn from years of housing compromised patients. A large open area, flanked with staff offices on the far end and patient rooms along a hallway on the opposite side, served as the common space.

The novelty of being committed to a psych ward momentarily sedated my paranoia. The nurse directed me to a room where a group of female patients were situated. My bed, one of six, was adjacent to the dingy wall. I sat on the edge of the bed while the nurse gave me a heavy dose of Thorazine. I don't remember if she injected me or gave me capsules. The conflict in my imagination subsided. For two days, I fell into a deep slumber devoid of any memorable dreams.

I awoke and vaguely remembered where I was. An aide peered into my room and insisted that I go to the common space. I reluctantly agreed and exited my room. I sat at a table nestled off to the side of the common space because I thought the other patients were conspiring against me. There I devoured a meal from a tray. A heavy, female patient from my room was swinging an object back and forth as she approached the common space. I imagined she was Madame Defarge, a forceful character depicted in *A Tale of Two Cities* by Charles Dickens. I was gripped with fear as, in my imagination, she summoned all the patients to revolt against me. I learned of an altercation between two patients in the ward, which made my paranoia increase. I was afraid of being attacked.

I was surrounded by patients from a different socioeconomic level. I couldn't see a way out of my situation, so I attempted to be invisible and did not connect with anyone or any activity. I spent three days on this unit, and then my father and Dr. Samuels arranged for my transfer to a psych ward at a private hospital where Dr. Samuels would counsel me.

The new unit had stark white walls and brightly colored doors to the patient rooms. Each room housed two patients. The hallway of rooms formed a U, with a multipurpose room spanning the bottom of the U. Therefore, the two hallways at each end of the U fed into the multipurpose room where patients ate and met with staff. Patients from a variety of economic backgrounds stayed in the unit. Several patients were addicted to drugs and alcohol, while others were plagued with mental conditions. Much like for me, the outside world became unbearable, and they were admitted to the hospital involuntarily. Adjacent to the large common space was a small room with arts and crafts, where I began crocheting.

At night all the patients assembled in the common space and watched television. Many of the patients smoked cigarettes in a designated room next to the staff offices, where medications were dispensed.

The psych ward was unlike anything I had imagined. I expected a cross between jail and a padded cell. On the contrary, the unit provided a place for patients to heal. We could talk about our situations and life at large (issues such as depression, mania, self-harm, mutilation, addictions, or our unstable lives in the outside world) with the aides and nurses. It was an oasis in the middle of a bustling society and afforded patients the opportunity to recover and reenter the world with a new medication regimen and coping skills.

I convened with Dr. Samuels a few times in addition to the doctor on staff in the unit. We skimmed the surface of my cyclic delusions. Although they subsided, the question was when these delusions would surface again from the depths of my plagued mind.

When I initially arrived at the new unit, I was still cagey and delusional. I imagined a revolt was taking place, and everyone I knew was abandoning me, leaving me to be persecuted in a desolate world. In the middle of the night, when everyone was sleeping, I rose from my bed. I quietly entered a male patient's room with a tube of toothpaste meant to be a peace offering. I believed the patient, Michael, was the spirit of my cousin because the two looked alike. Michael was startled, and he gently guided me back to my room without alerting the night staff. The next day we acted as if nothing had occurred, and we remained distant the entire time I was in the unit.

Every day I exercised, walking the hallways like I would an indoor track. I was friendly to everyone. Walking the halls and greeting everyone reminded me of my days in high school. Between classes, I had greeted the students like a politician seeking office. I wanted to be the most popular girl in my class. I was known as jovial and superfriendly, but I never developed deep friendships or a passion for intimacy in my teens. Therefore, no one got to know me. I maintained friendships on a superficial level but didn't connect to anyone, not even myself. How could I know anyone when I didn't know myself?

While in the unit, I did not feel the same tension or paranoia I had in the county psych ward. The bright walls and colorful doors in the newer facility contributed to the amiable atmosphere. I was in a euphoric state of mind. My life was improving, and I no longer felt like an object of scrutiny. My future was bright, and I felt hopefulness and positivity.

Every morning, I awoke from a glorious sleep, and my sanity was gradually returning. I applied my makeup and dressed as best as possible (my parents brought me a limited amount of clothing) before I went to the common room for breakfast. After breakfast, the staff and patients participated in a general floor meeting in the common room. We discussed issues such as cleaning up after meals, properly disposing of cigarette butts, and taking turns when choosing television programs. We were a miniature society while temporarily living together. The meeting lasted fifteen minutes, then everyone dispersed to continue with their morning activities: doctor's appointments, occupational therapy, discussion groups, art projects, and cooking.

Patients who were improving earned privileges such as leaving the locked unit to walk outside. I learned that the patients in the unit were everyday people whose emotional issues disrupted a stable existence. The unit became a haven from the tensions and irrational perceptions in a patient's life. Most patients were quiet and cooperated with the rules. A certain male patient who was about twenty-nine years old was the exception. He walked around the corridors, continually banging his head against the walls. He was uncontrollable and eventually stopped on his own. I wondered about his mental condition. Maybe he was hearing voices and couldn't dismiss the incessant noises in his head.

Every day I got stronger, and I was eager to return to life outside the ward. My parents visited at night. Mom was tentative and withdrawn. I felt her uncertainty. She had a daughter committed to a psych ward. Conversation was limited, but despite our silence, we chuckled at my situation. We made light of it.

I frequently avoided activities during the day and instead took long naps. I never skipped a meal; I was still recovering from days of not eating during my prolonged breakdown. I slowly gained the weight I had shed. My experience in the hospital was beneficial. I was able to sleep, and the stream of irrational thoughts subsided. I confronted my fears of being hospitalized, and it was not like the ward depicted in *One Flew Over the Cuckoo's Nest!* My illness was treated during a short stay in the unit. Thorazine, one of the first antipsychotic drugs on the market, made it possible for me to sleep after days without rest. The drug sedated my racing mind and arrested the judgmental, punishing thoughts I had about myself and my sexual history.

Since I was admitted to the locked unit involuntarily, I remained there for three weeks before the doctors deemed me rational enough to reenter the outside world.

I met with Dr. Samuels a few times while I was in the private hospital. He still did not seem to understand my cyclic condition. He never addressed my pattern of paranoia and other symptoms, such as sleep deprivation, which led to my breakdown. Becoming educated and aware of these patterns that developed from social stresses would have helped me cope after a cycle began, but Dr. Samuels never enlightened me.

CHAPTER 13

Doctors released me from the hospital psych ward in mid-September 1980, and I withdrew from school since I had missed so many classes. I worked part-time for my father and impatiently began searching for an apartment in a nearby town. My dream was to live independently. I had lost contact with Ron. He had witnessed my fall from normalcy firsthand, and his cold, judgmental father had probably instructed him to avoid me. My illness and I were trouble and had no place in their conventional world.

In October, I purchased a Pekingese puppy. Dad and I discovered an ad in the local paper about a litter of Pekingese puppies available for purchase. The breeder lived in eastern Long Island, which was about an hour away. The breeder was an older, stout, disheveled woman who lived in a dingy house. The puppy didn't have any documents, but that didn't deter us from paying $250 for her. The breeder instructed me to take good care of the pup and to make her my priority every day. The puppy was small yet feisty. I named her Ming Lee. Dad hoped that, by taking care of a life other than my own, I'd find some stability and self-esteem.

I was back in touch with Roger, the student from the Middle East. We remained friends despite our cultural differences and my secret double life. One day, Roger visited me at home. I immediately introduced him to Ming Lee, and he met my parents as well. They silently disapproved of my relationship with Roger. He was taken with my home and called it "paradise on the water's edge." He joked that if we ever moved out, he'd be the first one to purchase it.

Even though I longed to be Roger's girlfriend, his loyalty to his father outweighed his feelings for me. As a Jewish girl, I simply wasn't accepted by his Christian family in the Middle East. I didn't realize at the time that he risked his familial ties by being my friend. We were never intimate, but our friendship was solid. Had he ever learned of my illness, breakdowns, and psych ward committals, I'm sure he would have dropped me like a hot potato and never looked back.

I finally found a one-bedroom apartment in a Long Island co-op, about thirty minutes from home. Animals were not allowed, so I hid Ming Lee. The apartment was on the second floor of a three-story, garden apartment. It was a corner apartment at the end of a narrow hallway and adjacent to a fire exit. I used the fire-exit stairs to take Ming Lee for walks. She was a huge responsibility, and I neglected to fully house-train her. I adored her cuteness, but she required much more care than I was giving her. Both of us suffered.

The apartment was adequate for my needs as a single woman living alone. A long, open area functioned as the dining and living rooms. A large window overlooked the small parking lot below. The kitchen, bathroom, and bedroom were parallel to the dining/living room. The apartment faced east, so in the morning, sunlight flooded through the window, but as the day progressed, the rooms got dimmer and needed artificial lighting.

I furnished the apartment with items from my parents' house: white leather and chrome chairs and a chartreuse sofa with a floral print. A colorful area rug added a comfy accent to the contemporary decor. The dining space, directly next to the entrance to the apartment, remained empty. I kept a small, round table and some chairs in the worn kitchen, where the appliances needed to be replaced. I set up my drafting desk in the corner of my bedroom adjacent to a window that overlooked the parking lot. In time, I developed steady work habits since only Ming Lee was there to distract me. My twin bed provided just enough room for the two of us.

When I moved into the apartment, an overzealous man in his early thirties welcomed me to the co-op. He resembled his idol, Bruce Springsteen. The neighbor's name was Elliot, and he lived in the apartment directly above me. Elliot was an accountant for the Internal Revenue Service. His eyes were blue and cold as steel. He wanted sex without the trappings of a relationship. Vying to conquer me was a game to him. His fiancée, whom he adored, had broken off their engagement while Elliot's father was dying. Elliot's latent anger festered, and he was inclined to be mean-spirited. He falsely led me to believe he was interested in my welfare.

Elliot constantly tried to lure me into having sex with him, and he showed me his pristine, renovated apartment and king-size bed. When Elliot revealed to me the details of his father's death, we were sitting together in his kitchen. He was drunk, clutching a bottle of hard liquor. I felt so sorry for him. I wanted to hug him, but I knew better than to make physical contact. Elliot subtly steered his resentment toward me because *my* father was still alive. Despite that, I became quite fond of Elliot, and it took all my strength to rebuff his physical advances. He always flirted with, teased, and challenged me. He frequently strolled down the fire-exit stairs and knocked on my door. He asked if I was ready for his passion. He was slowly breaking down my wall of abstinence.

I invited Roger to see my apartment. When he arrived at my door, Elliot quickly flew down the fire-exit stairs to get a look at the man I adored. When I opened the door, I was startled to see Elliot's face, and I shooed him away. Roger was baffled about this other man in my life, and I was annoyed and embarrassed. Elliot behaved like he had control over my life. Who was this nosy man who seemed to demand all of me? I was flattered but mostly annoyed as he inserted himself between me and Roger, the man I wanted more than anything in this world.

Elliot made disruptive noises from his apartment— stomping and playing loud music—and Roger wondered what Elliot meant to me. He alluded that I should date Elliot. I was outraged and embarrassed by the loud noise coming from the ceiling. It felt like an invasion of my privacy.

We sat in the living room, and I told Roger I was returning to college in the spring. It would be my last semester, and then I had plans to work at an architecture firm. Roger aspired to own a construction company in the city after graduation. He had another year to finish. I listened patiently to Roger. I appreciated him making the long trek from the city to see my apartment, and the more he avoided intimacy with me, the more I wanted him. Now that I had my own space, I desperately wanted to go further with Roger, but he avoided any sexual contact with me. He looked around my apartment, commended it, and wished me the best of luck.

CHAPTER 14

The spring semester of 1981 arrived. I enrolled in design, environmental design construction documents, and two electives. I was committed to a full schedule and ready to finish the architecture program I started back in 1974. In one of my classes, I met a female architecture student named Yvonne, who came from Ireland. She had dark hair, a fair complexion, and brilliant, sparkling blue-green eyes. She was my height, and her speech was elegantly tinted with a slight brogue. We became friends and enjoyed Manhattan. I kept my psychotic condition hidden from her. The way Ron and his family reacted to my previous breakdown confirmed my certainty that no one would understand or accept me.

Yvonne lived in lower Manhattan in an apartment she eventually purchased with the inheritance her father had left her. She had four sisters who lived all over the world and a half brother named Tom; he lived in Virginia and frequently visited New York. Tom was about fifteen years older than we were and was the son from Yvonne's father's first marriage. He didn't resemble Yvonne at all. Tom was totally infatuated with me. I didn't realize it at the time, which was unfortunate, as his affection would have lifted my spirits. He adored how I dressed and especially liked my fuzzy, pink sweater that I wore often. It accentuated my body yet still left something to the imagination. I would have loved Tom's attentiveness, but we were too far apart in age, and he did not want more children, which I desperately yearned for. Four sons were enough for him. Even though I did not fully realize his sentiments, his flattery helped my self-image.

I visited Yvonne at her apartment many times. She played host to lavish dinner parties for her intimate crowd of friends and Peter, her devoted boyfriend. He was English and employed in Manhattan. Her apartment brimmed with color. The walls were painted orange, and the molding around the windows was stark white. The corner studio apartment provided grand views of lower Manhattan that were perfect for dinner parties.

Yvonne was considerate and fun-loving. I learned a lot about etiquette from her. For instance, she would call me the day after we spent time together and communicate how much she enjoyed my company. Her manners and views about life were sophisticated and compassionate, unlike the acquaintances of my past. Although Yvonne demonstrated immense consideration for others, it was too much to ask her to understand my cycle of madness. When I was well, I functioned normally and found accepting my reality of breaking down difficult. Due to my denial, I could not protect myself and avoid the next downward spiral into the dungeon of insanity. I did speak to Yvonne about Roger though. I confessed I was stuck on him even though we couldn't be in a relationship. Nothing compared to the blissful, passionate six months that we dated before Roger fell under his father's rule and authority.

Yvonne and I were enrolled in the same environmental design class. The professor was dedicated to his agenda and conveyed to the class the impact nature had on a structural design. We learned about Earth's ecosystems and how vital it was to understand how the soils would support the foundation of a building or a city. We learned the implications of exposure and orientation when designing a building. Together, we became more sensitive to the environment in an urban context as well as the open countryside. We studied the great twentieth-century architects Frank Lloyd Wright and Louis Kahn and how their buildings implemented environmental considerations. Alvar Aalto and Le Corbusier were also impressive contextual designers who were sensitive to nature and incorporated the environment into their creations. The shape of their structures took into account the sun, wind, soil type, and surrounding area—lakes, mountains, forests, sand, or city.

In design studio, my last class before graduation, the assigned project was to design a multi-use, high-rise complex consisting of apartments, a community center, and commercial stores. I was confident I could succeed. I designed a sculptural high-rise that included twenty-four stories of residential apartments. Each floor had an open, triangular-shaped corner balcony for communal use. A community center and theater comprised the first six floors, which protruded beyond the façade of the residential tower.

During the final week of the semester, we presented our designs in the large common room in the architecture building. I was anxious to display my project because my drawings of floor plans and elevations were light and difficult to read from a moderate distance. I surveyed the walls that held all our projects and saw many bold, professional presentations that were extremely legible from any distance in the room.

I wanted to flee immediately. I watched as students lectured about their projects with stellar devotion. They brimmed with confidence, as if they knew their designs were more than adequate. I knew their designs were less creative than mine, but their drawings were vibrant and accurate. Anyone could grasp the ideas and format of their designs. I failed to realize the drawings were as important as the design and counted for half the grade.

Suddenly, it was my turn, and I moved slowly to my drawings, sweating profusely. I stood to the side of my presentation and did not dare look at the audience of professors and students. Our professor hammered me for presenting illegible drawings.

I wanted to run away, much like I had run away from a large, stray dog in an open school field when I was seven years old. I kept running and running, fearing the dog would attack me. Finally, I reached the end of the field, and the gym teacher chased away the dog. I felt conspicuous and embarrassed. I imagined the class of seven-year-old students were laughing at me. I wanted to hide and disappear.

My heart pounded furiously as the professor remarked that I achieved a creative design, but no one could decipher its quality due to the pale, tentative drawings. If I presented my design to a client, I would fail. I cringed with embarrassment as the entire room looked at me with disdain. My creative efforts took a backseat to my failure to communicate the design through my drawings. I avoided looking at the crowded room and stared at my inadequate project, which I continued to believe was terrifically complex.

The professor assigned an incomplete grade, so I had to redo my drawings to pass the class. At least the actual design could remain intact. I was fortunate the professor didn't fail me for my incomplete presentation, and I had the opportunity to correct the situation. I had the chance to redeem myself.

The professor was below my height and brimming with stern discipline. He was extremely professional. Even though my drawings were an improvement compared to my first attempt, he was critical and forcefully told me that no architecture firm would hire me as a draftsman or designer. I asked if he would hire me, and he responded curtly, "Absolutely not." I felt his words and rejection punch me in the chest. He said I had to get my act together and work hard on improving my drafting skills. The professor erased my sense of success in executing a creative design by commenting that my project was socialistic and not economically viable in the capitalistic society where each space had to be monetarily productive. Despite his harsh criticism, the professor granted me a passing grade.

I also had to complete a set of construction drawings—a design of a library—for my building documents class. The professor was older and kinder than my design professor, and he was patient and polite as we reviewed the foundation plans, wall and window details, cross sections, and floor plans.

I finally earned a professional degree in architecture in the summer of 1981. Since I was a late graduate, I didn't have a celebration or attend the graduation ceremony in the spring. I was elated that I had finally crossed the finish line. My satisfaction didn't endure, however, since the design professor's sharp words rang in my ears and made me question my self-worth again. Graduating was bittersweet. I didn't graduate with flying colors and struggled to the bitter end in achieving my long-awaited degree.

CHAPTER 15

Elliot continued his bombardment of flirty behavior and demanded I succumb to his sexual fantasies. Despite this, I believed he sincerely wanted a more meaningful relationship. One night, when I was still feeling dejected from the merciless words of my design professor, I knocked on Elliot's door wearing only a trench coat.

He gleefully invited me in, and I dropped my coat, revealing my body to a very surprised Elliot. He was stunned to see me offer myself after he had pursued me for so long. I wanted passionate sex, and he obliged. One night turned into a physical marathon, and I thought it was the beginning of a committed relationship.

I wanted Elliot to be my boyfriend and for us to eventually get married, but I was merely a conquest for Elliot. When he was satiated and satisfied with winning his game of many months, his interest in me diminished significantly. He never realized that I loved him, and I kept my true feelings hidden since I was afraid of his potential rejection.

Elliot held onto his anger from his broken engagement, and I couldn't compete with the memory of his dear fiancée. He was contemptuous and took me for granted. At the time, it never occurred to me that I meant little to him. Perhaps he thought I was involved with Roger. Unfortunately, Elliot's respect for me plummeted, and I felt degraded and unworthy.

I had been the rebound girl, and he was unable to recognize that a nice Jewish girl not only felt passion for him but also wanted a serious commitment. I truly cared about him, but he wallowed in his broken engagement. I berated myself for having sex with Elliot. I took the entire event personally instead of understanding that he was immature and shallow.

In time, we became strangers, as if nothing had ever occurred between us. By his actions of ignoring me after our physical, lustful sex, I assumed he thought I was loose. But what about *him*? He indulged in sex more than I did. He told me he had relations with another woman every week.

CHAPTER 16

Yvonne's dinner parties were elegant and enjoyable, and I reminded myself that I could find Mr. Right at any moment. During one such party, Yvonne's close friend, a tall, slender woman whose husband was dutifully beside her, spoke about her recent excursion to Greece. She highlighted her trip to the Parthenon, on the ancient site of the Acropolis, where the origins of democracy and Western architecture began centuries ago.

The following day, I decided to book a seven-day tour of mainland Greece and a week-long excursion to Club Med, a resort on an island in the Aegean Sea. The travel agent remarked that this trip would be too stressful for any individual, especially one traveling alone. A seven-day tour was enough, and I could return to Club Med at another time.

Nothing could deter me from exploring Greece. I let my love of history and longing to travel outweigh concerns about my mental health. Despite my history of breaking down when the social environment became stressful, Dr. Samuels did not caution me against traveling to Greece.

My devoted father escorted me to the airport three weeks later. He was hesitant to let me go since he noticed my behavior was askew. My eyes were glassy, and my gaze appeared unfocused. He might have sensed something was off, but I was obstinate and yearned for an adventure thousands of miles away.

I sat in an aisle seat on the huge plane. On my left sat an amiable, middle-aged woman who also had plans to tour Greece. Her husband was seated in the row behind us. I conversed openly with the woman and revealed the personal depths of my lonely crusade. I spoke of my failed relationship and my endless search to find a mate. As she listened to my woes, the friendly lady lifted the armrest between us, allowing us to share personal space. I began to feel ill at ease, as though I had betrayed my privacy and modesty. My feelings of inadequacy and promiscuity surfaced as my personal confessions crossed the boundary of propriety. Despite this stranger's compassion for me, my delusions of being an outcast loomed larger than ever. A tingling paranoia began to emerge.

The plane finally landed, and we traveled separately to our hotels. Since this was a unique, novel adventure, I suppressed my demons and tried to enjoy the trip. The next morning, the friendly couple met me at the base of the Acropolis, and we climbed to the plateau that overlooked the city of Athens.

The Acropolis, constructed two thousand years ago, remained partially intact despite being subjected to numerous wars. The enormity of the Parthenon made me feel like a peanut standing in its shadow. Gargantuan, fluted columns formed a colonnade on each façade. The Greeks constructed the temple to house the statue of Athena for all citizens to observe and revere. The architect embraced detail and mathematical harmony. The site was breathtaking.

Our conversation was limited as we progressed in our sightseeing. We acknowledged that we felt like specks in the universe among such iconic and ancient wonders. My formal tour started the next day, and I never encountered the friendly couple again.

A diverse group of tourists congregated at the designated hotel in Athens, ready for a guided tour of Greece. Eastern Europeans, Swedes, an elderly American couple, a French couple, and a middle-aged gentleman from America formed our group of about twenty. I was the youngest and had little in common with the others, particularly the foreigners who spoke in their own languages.

I decided to befriend the American gentleman, who also seemed lonely. His name was Edward, and he was a rotund, Irish-looking fellow who donned a beret. We sat together in the rear of the bus for the duration of the tour. Even though Edward was decades my senior, I had no choice but to rely on his friendship.

The tour guide was a petite brunette who spoke in scholarly detail about the ruins of mainland Greece. These talks provoked a romantic vision of the past, two thousand years ago. At the beginning of the tour, I enthusiastically romanticized the history of carnage, war, and cultural beauty from centuries ago. This infatuation did not last after I grew fatigued, and insomnia gradually plagued my stability. The tedious tour consistently made three or four stops per day. As the tour progressed, every ancient site started to look the same—filled with stone, rubble, green pastures, Doric columns, and archways. Each night, our tour group retired at a different hotel, so I practically lived out of my suitcase to avoid unpacking and repacking daily. The insomnia got worse day by day and so did my attention to hygiene and dress protocol.

One of the hotels was situated dramatically atop a cliff and had a gorgeous view of the pure, blue sea. The shores were specked with white buildings that glimmered when the sun hit them and faded as the sun withdrew.

I inhaled the crisp air from the balcony of my room. I longed to be with Roger and share this romantic vista with him. I lay in the bed restless, frustrated, and alone. The beautiful view was pointless without him. Nothing mattered without Roger.

Halfway through the tour, we stopped for lunch at a café that offered authentic Greek food. I sat at a table with Edward and the French couple in a simple dining room. The tables were covered with pristine, white tablecloths, and hints of blue and green appeared everywhere. I was on the verge of picking up a succulent orange near my plate when the gaunt, French lady who sat across from me quickly snatched it out of my reach. She began to fiercely lick the skin of the orange while glaring at me with angry, resentful eyes. It seemed as though she could not tolerate my civil and friendly manner toward her husband, who was seated next to me. Neither Edward nor I reacted to the woman's bizarre behavior. It was if she was exhibiting hatred for Americans. We were stupefied and ignored this unnerving demonstration of abhorrent manners while her husband kept talking and ignoring his wife's childish behavior.

I felt dire loneliness and started to believe everyone was conspiring against me. I struggled to coexist with these strangers, and Edward's friendship was not enough to get me through. Another night without sleep followed. It was the fifth day on this endless tour, and I lagged behind the group.

While everyone was boarding the bus early one morning, I stayed in my hotel room to take a bath. I believed that if I were preoccupied, the tour group would leave without me, and I would be free to return to Athens. My scheme was fruitless because our tour guide, who was responsible for the safety of all the tourists, would not abandon me. She feared for my well-being and for her job. This petite, authoritative guide summoned me back to the bus. I felt trapped. The hot bath induced menstruation, and I was not wearing any protection. I bled through my undergarments and felt embarrassed as I remained frozen in my seat on the bus. Once the tour reached the next hotel, I immediately went to my assigned room and cleansed myself. I also retrieved the sanitary napkins buried in my suitcase.

Another night without sleep resulted. It was the sixth day, and the end of the hellish tour was near. We visited Delphi, where an ancient temple dedicated to the Greek god Apollo, son of Zeus, was erected more than two thousand years prior. This place of worship overlooked a rocky valley. Despite my paranoia, I was moved by the beauty of Delphi and the magnificent terrain outside of the bus window. I remained frozen in my seat though, while the rest of the group ascended the picturesque foothills. As I gazed through the window, I imagined it was a porthole in a sinking ship. I saw my parents' faces chiseled into the stone foothills, and their facial features shook like leaves fluttering in the wind. I imagined their spirits lurking in the hallowed grounds as they departed from the earth. I was abandoned and left to fend for myself in a desolate land, weary and fatigued, a prisoner unable to escape.

Suddenly, I experienced a revelation. I had to be betrothed. I could face the world and conquer my demons if I had a partner to validate my existence. I got out of my seat and walked to the front of the bus. I approached the bus driver, who was idly waiting for the group to return. He glanced in my direction and was mildly startled by my proximity and raggedy appearance. I mustered all my courage and asked the bus driver if he would marry me. How could he deny me when I was so earnest? He froze and looked both annoyed and concerned for his job, which was counter to my expectations. I never thought he would refuse my proposal. He marched me back to my seat and delivered a loud, panic-driven response. He could lose his job if I kept this up! I sank into my seat, feeling like my wings had been clipped and my revelation shattered.

Oddly, I wasn't embarrassed about this failed mission. I returned to gazing out the window as if nothing had transpired, and I was back to the beginning of my search for Mr. Right. I had suffered for days without food, sleep, or the ability to distinguish fantasy from reality. The group finally returned to the bus, and we continued our journey to a port town. No one found out about my proposal.

During the early evening in the port town, I sat wearily on a park bench in a courtyard near an anchored cruise ship. The intimate group of Eastern Europeans from my tour sat nearby, reveling in their conversation and ignoring me.

Their rude dismissal of my presence reminded me of when I was a toddler, and my mother enrolled me in nursery school two weeks after the session had started. I felt isolated because the youngsters had formed their friendships already, so when they went outside to play in the sandbox, I remained in the empty classroom along with a blind student. Her eyes were as white as the purity of God's light: no iris, no pupil, just a sea of white. I was traumatized by this sight, and the memory of being isolated and fraught with fear lasted many years.

The tour guide, who probably pitied me, invited me to shop in the port town. I foolishly turned down her gracious invitation and stayed rooted to the bench. I wanted to board the cruise ship and travel across the sea to Israel: a country, a haven, and a respite for a Jewish American. I eventually returned to my hotel room, where the decrepit air conditioner hummed loudly and generated stale air. Another night of sleep eluded me. The following morning, we returned to Athens. It seemed an eternity had passed.

In the beginning of embracing this foreign land, I was innocent to my underlying limitation in coping with a tour that entailed a challenging social situation and its repetitive arduous journey of ancient Greece. The daily regimen of complex, scholarly lectures was more tedious than I had expected.

Before the tour group disbanded, the two Swedish women approached me. They were nurses and privy to my insomnia. They offered to give me medication that would help me sleep. I adamantly refused their help because I was scared that the medication would make me unconscious for days—I hadn't slept for five nights, and my body and mind were fighting a battle of illusory thoughts. I was quivering and on the edge of imploding from insanity.

The room I stayed in that night was old and oppressive like the room in the port town. The air conditioner rattled, and the mattress was thin. I tossed and turned as my mind raced with punitive thoughts, and any semblance of reason that surfaced among the murky waters of my brain were strangled. About midnight, I could not bear it any longer. I left my room and climbed to the roof of the hotel. Once I reached the top of the stairs and passed through the heavy door, I continued walking slowly to the edge of the roof. I stood by the parapet wall and embraced the dramatic view of Athens while the night air momentarily soothed my fractured soul.

The concierge stood near me smoking a cigarette. I asked him what he was thinking about. He responded with a curt smile and implored me to return to the safety of my room.

I returned to my room, but I was again unsuccessful in quieting my mind. I could not stop thinking and punishing myself for imagined transgressions of my past. I could not forgive myself and find solace in the painful moment. To escape my hell, I vacated my room, left the hotel, and walked the desolate streets of Athens. People were asleep in their beds, and all of Athens was closed for the night. A Greek soldier approached me and politely asked if I had a light for his cigarette. I was amazed he would even speak to me since I appeared so soiled and disheveled. Unsure of his motives, I responded by softly saying I had none but wished I could help. He then asked me if he could join my walk of the unoccupied streets of Athens. Some of the neighborhoods were less than favorable, and I was astonished that this stranger, who appeared out of nowhere, saved me from any imminent danger that might have been lurking around the corner. We silently walked for several hours before he escorted me back to my hotel, and we parted forever.

It was dawn. For a brief interlude, I felt relieved about surviving Athens with a caring stranger who simply accepted my company with no regard or obligation for the future or the past. As I returned to my guest room, I realized I had to return to New York and abandon my plans to head to Club Med. I grabbed my suitcase, checked out of the dingy hotel, hailed a cab, and proceeded to the airport in an agitated state. I was anxious to return home.

I managed to navigate the bustling airport on autopilot, my body and mind feverishly searching for an airport attendant who could help me. I frantically lugged my suitcase to a counter, briefed an attendant that I was ill and had to return home, and as luck would have it, I was on the next flight to New York.

CHAPTER 17

This time, on my journey home, I sat by a window, which I didn't even bother to use. My interest in Greece no longer existed. A woman about my age sat next to me, and I found her proximity and sheer presence disconcerting. Her father, who was seated in the row ahead of us, turned toward me and feebly attempted to converse with me and coerce me into talking to his daughter. I ignored his efforts, and he became frustrated with my silence. His irate words increased my feelings of isolation and paranoia. He finally gave up and turned around in his seat.

Left in silence, I listened to the conversation between two men who were sitting behind me. My deluded mind imagined that they were insulting me and my appearance. I automatically stood up and turned around to face them. Their conversation abruptly ceased as they gazed at my disheveled appearance. I stared back at them, then slapped the face of the man seated directly behind me for offending my reputation and dignity. The gentleman was stunned, and the passengers froze in shock. A scary moment passed as I'm sure they wondered whether a brawl would occur. I left my seat in a hurry and ran down the aisle toward the front of the plane. I stumbled up the stairs to the second level where the first-class cabin was.

The space was luxurious, accommodating the rich and famous. In the first row of seats, near the stairs, sat a famous pop singer and her bodyguard. I grabbed a vacant seat a row behind them and felt overcome with relief that no one followed me. I did not realize the seriousness of what I had just done. The flight attendant allowed me to remain in the first-class cabin so as not to disrupt the privileged passengers. The staff probably surmised I was tripping on drugs and would pass out. They were ignorant and inexperienced in recognizing a mental breakdown. The symptoms of my illness were rare and often misdiagnosed in 1981. Displays of paranoia were usually attributed to hallucinogens, and society could not fathom I had a mental illness that had nothing to do with drugs (although angel dust had spurred my cycles of insanity back in 1977).

The bodyguard with the pop singer reached out and held my hand. He was handsome and sturdy and asked me if I liked the Grateful Dead. I was vaguely familiar with the popular band and replied, "Sure, I do." He probably thought I was into mind-altering drugs like the band was.

The plane finally landed, and the flight attendant directed me to stay in my seat while all the other passengers vacated. Then the Port Authority police came. I was fearful and shocked when they handcuffed me like a dangerous criminal. They took me to the transportation police station. I was calm and submissive. That was the only time I had been arrested. A large police officer informed me that the gentleman I slapped was, luckily, not pressing any criminal charges against me. As I sat on the bench inside the police station, the burly police officer was kind enough to place a jacket over the handcuffs, so I didn't look like a common criminal. I meekly asked the officer to summon my father. I realized I needed to consult with Dr. Samuels before I slid even further into insanity. I was relieved to see my father arrive at the station. An officer released me from the handcuffs and custody. Dad never found out what crime I committed. The police officer observed how happy he was that I was alive and decided to remain silent on the cause of my arrest.

Dad and I headed to Dr. Samuels' office. I'm sure Dad feared he would have to hold me back from escaping like he had before, but contrary to his expectations, I remained calm and anticipated a productive session with the doctor.

Ever since Joseph had given me angel dust, my breakdowns were more frequent. They occurred every six months to a year, and my poor parents got no rest. They slept in their clothes like soldiers in battle. They prayed for a solution to my irrational cycles but got no respite, only a flickering ray of hope at the end of a long, delirious tunnel when I might return to normal.

When we arrived, I didn't say anything to Dr. Samuels for fear I would end up once more in a psych ward or worse. To break the silence, Dr. Samuels inappropriately remarked that I had nice legs. I felt cheap and found his flattery offensive. My hair was straggly, my clothes were soiled, my face was dirty, and I had shadows beneath my eyes, but somehow, the doctor thought I was healthy and alert. He could not crack the veneer of distrust I had for him and took my silence to mean I was well enough to return to my life in New York. Dad took me back to my apartment and stayed with me for the night. We had a light dinner at a diner next to my apartment. The familiar landscape soothed my unsteady mind some, and I finally ate a bit before we retired to my apartment.

Mom continued taking care of Ming Lee as she had during my trip overseas. Dad settled himself on the couch in my living room. I returned to my bedroom, still finding it impossible to fall asleep since the low dose of Thorazine Dr. Samuels had just prescribed was not enough to induce slumber. It was still better to be restless in my own bed than stranded in the heart of Athens. I waited until my father was asleep to quietly exit the apartment. I took the fire-exit stairs up to the roof but hesitated walking out onto it for risk of falling. The view from the roof wasn't as spectacular as the city of Athens, only a sullen sky above the suburban street below. I was finished with running away. I needed to battle my demons. I decided to return to my apartment.

On my way back down the stairs, I stopped on the third floor and knocked lightly on Elliot's door. I got no response. He either wasn't there or was sleeping too deeply to hear me. I wondered what his reaction would be to me showing up in the middle of the night. I was sparsely dressed in night clothes and seeking comfort.

Disappointed yet relieved, I returned to my apartment. Dad remained asleep. By some miracle, I dozed off into a light slumber and broke my cycle of insomnia. My fears of waking up to a deserted world and the same episodic, imaginary revolution subsided.

The next morning arrived, and Dad had no clue what had transpired in the night. He and Dr. Samuels concluded it would be best for me to stay at my parents' house for two weeks. I slowly gained stability; my sleep improved day by day and my feelings of isolation and paranoia abated. After two weeks in a structured environment, with three meals a day and my caring parents, I was able to return to my apartment and resume my life; however, we decided Ming Lee should live with my parents.

The owner of my apartment doubled the cost of the monthly rent when the lease was to renew in November, so I sought a co-op apartment that my parents eventually purchased. I left my neighbor Elliot behind. He fulfilled my physical passion but not my need for affection and commitment. Things might have been different if only I had informed him of my love for him, but the powerful phrase never surfaced. Our paths never crossed again, and I forged ahead with my hunt for Mr. Right.

Meanwhile, a prestigious architecture firm hired me as a draftsman. The firm was in a small town near the Long Island Sound. My seven years of education finally led me to employment in the architecture field.

My assignments included simple drafting tasks, such as designing title pages for several projects. I got bored quickly and wanted more challenging work. I engaged in frequent conversations with an ambitious draftsman, Charles, who sat adjacent to my desk. He had been with the firm for two years and worked on complex drafting assignments.

Charles had dark, thick hair and dark eyes to match. He was determined in his work. We spoke of our college years and our travels, and I was negligent in completing the simple, repetitive work assigned to me. I was unaware that if I put in the time and performed with excellence, I would eventually obtain more meaningful work.

Charles realized my glaring incompetence over time, and we became resentful of each other. Our conversations became abrasive and distracted the drafting team who sat near us. The manager eventually noticed the disruptive bickering between Charles and me.

Nothing deterred me from attending work each day, but my demons were beating my door again. I began to feel isolated. I was going through the motions of everyday life without being invested.

The co-op apartment was much nicer than my previous rental. It was a one-bedroom apartment on the top floor of a three-story building, and it had plenty of light. Every feature seemed bright and new—recently painted walls, a parquet floor, tiled floor in the kitchen, and new appliances. I kept most of the furniture from my previous apartment and purchased a taupe laminate bureau, a queen-size bed, and a contemporary, tan cloth sectional. The bedroom closet was huge and enabled plenty of storage for my many shopping sprees. I didn't save my money, and I constantly replenished my wardrobe. I was fortunate that my parents were able to purchase this beautiful apartment for me. The deed was in my mother's name, and when they sold the apartment, Mom reaped a generous profit.

My dog, Ming Lee, could live with me again. I didn't have to hide her in a bag anymore just to take her for walks. With the apartment came a new routine. I worked, visited my parents, and spent time with Ming Lee.

I had a convenient parking spot in the garage. Every day, I noticed a beautiful, yellow Porsche parked near my little, yellow car. One day, I met the owner of the vehicle. He was a man about eight years my senior. He was tall with a tawny complexion and unexpressive brown eyes. His hair was slightly gray, but he was also balding. From the moment we encountered each other, I knew an insipid relationship would ensue. He was available and made it known. I was impatient in finding Mr. Right, so I settled on this man whose chemistry only mildly attracted me.

His name was Morty, which suited his bland personality. He rented an apartment on the first floor and struggled with his monthly expenses because he was an unemployed lawyer. I believed he could easily find employment since he earned his degree from an Ivy League college. Morty asked me out. I accepted even though it meant tolerating his nasally voice and average demeanor. He even had a comb-over. I gradually learned that Morty incessantly sought "the job." He wanted a perfect situation, which caused him to experience long stretches of unemployment. His parents had moved to Florida, so he lacked the support of his family.

Morty and I became closer and intimate. I ignored the underlying current that told me I was settling out of desperation for a man, that my ravenous, romantic fire had been doused. Despite my lack of enthusiasm, Morty offered security and companionship when I had difficulty living alone.

In a span of just three weeks, and without much thought, Morty moved into my apartment. I believed our relationship was becoming serious, but Morty's intentions and sentiments were not mutual. I blatantly revealed that I wanted to get married in the future and was naive to Morty's motives. He moved into my apartment because he had no job and could not contribute to the monthly co-op maintenance. I was so infatuated with the idea of living together that I neglected to realize the inequality between our financial situations. I had a job and familial support, whereas Morty owned only a beautiful car that he eventually sold.

My job situation did not improve, and eventually the office manager fired me. My self-esteem took a hit, but I didn't care about the job since it was going nowhere.

CHAPTER 18

Morty didn't want to live with my adorable little dog, Ming Lee. He claimed he had allergies to the dog's dander. Ming Lee moved in with my parents, and I had to part with my loyal friend. Succumbing to Morty's dislike of Ming Lee and being fired from my first drafting job weighed heavily on my conscience and caused my demons to surface. The feelings of being unwanted and undesirable returned. Unfortunately, Morty's alliance with me could not equate to the unconditional love Ming Lee and I shared.

I felt like I had failed at everything so early in life. Morty didn't understand my despair or predicament and instead regarded me as unusual while he dealt with his own unemployment. He lacked any compassion for me, yet I clung to him to avoid my loneliness.

On a crisp winter evening in March 1982, I had an attack of paranoia, and I clumsily put on my black winter jacket and my shoes and left the apartment. I felt disconnected, and the familiar surroundings seemed foreign. I was outside of myself and numb to any external activities. I had to run away. I ran to the laundry room in the basement of the co-op building. I took off my shoes and coat and left them there. I walked through town to an area of secluded houses and then made my way to a park several miles away, by the Long Island Sound.

I was an alien seeking new land. I desperately wanted to begin life again since I was mourning the reckless passing of my youth.

Meanwhile, Morty contacted my parents to let them know about my strange behavior and that he found my shoes and winter jacket in the laundry room. If Morty had loved me, he would have searched for me. But I was just a convenience to him. My parents notified the police I was missing. My cycle of delusion was occurring again, and I had no power to arrest it and return to normalcy. I was alone, and I felt like a refugee walking the streets, with no ties or connection.

The skies were clear and windy. The soles of my feet began to ache as I stood still by the water's edge and silently pondered the meaning of my life. My spirit was oscillating and steering me toward a life devoid of any reason and peace. I tore myself away from the seashore and continued to walk.

I was wandering aimlessly when the local police spotted me. They gently took hold of me, but I resisted. They formed a line of three officers and held me horizontally. Each officer held onto a different part of my body as they passed me into the backseat of the police car. They asked me what my name was, and I answered with a fictitious name. I tried relentlessly to conceal my identity while they took me to the private hospital where I had recently been treated. The authorities summoned Dad to the emergency room to identify me, and I was admitted once again to the psych ward, a place I was now familiar with. The medical staff placed me in a locked room.

I sat motionless on the edge of the bed and gazed into space in a catatonic state. Morty peered through the window of the locked door and laughed at me. He had no affection and love for his girlfriend, who was suffering in the middle of a meltdown. I continued to sit upright, motionless and stoic. A nurse entered the room and administered a heavy dose of Thorazine in pill form, which I swallowed without a struggle. I gradually fell into a deep slumber that lasted several days, and the symptoms of my psychosis subsided. I finally awoke and participated in the regimen of the psych ward.

Morty visited and brought me a flower. The interaction between us was awkward. I suppose he had never encountered a person who suffered so much from a mental disorder. After scouring the ward for some semblance of a vase, he managed to find a plastic urinal. He quipped that the urinal was very fitting for me. I found his words and actions tasteless and disturbing. The urinal reminded me of middle school, when I rendered a drawing of a cactus plant that looked like a gigantic penis. The drawing was superb, but I negated my accomplishment because I was embarrassed by my depiction of a glaring phallic symbol.

Morty did not visit me again. Perhaps he thought he was entitled to live in my apartment because he tolerated my mental disorder. He treated me like a second-class citizen to be taken advantage of. I realized he didn't care about me. All he cared about was his own survival.

After two weeks, I left the hospital and went to my parents' house for another two weeks. I was fully recuperated when I returned to my apartment. Morty didn't offer an affectionate welcome, nor did he express gratitude for being able to live in my apartment during my absence. When we dined out, we split the bill. Not once did he offer to treat. After he sold his yellow Porsche, he was able to coast on the profit for a little while. He began contributing to the monthly maintenance fee for the apartment. Together, we opened a joint savings account and began to accrue a small amount of funds.

The dull days were passed slowly as Morty continued his search for the ideal job. Finally, another architecture firm in downtown Manhattan hired me. I had to take the train and the subway, which made for a long, arduous commute. Again, I drafted site plans, a miniscule part of the building project. Again, I was too talkative with my coworkers who sat nearby. Again, I wanted to be a designer, the most sought-after position in an architecture firm, and again, I was brimming with the impatience that inhibited me in every endeavor. I wanted to be a designer immediately, without acquiring the necessary experience. My goals in the architecture world were unreachable as far as I was concerned. I did not take seriously the simple tasks I was assigned, and I continued a pattern of talking to my neighboring drafters I encountered in the firm.

In spring 1982, Morty and I took a trip to Philadelphia to visit his college roommate, Harold. His friend was a tall, slender, serious man who was married and expecting his first child. I could sense Morty felt displaced since he had not achieved what Harold had. This accomplished friend was employed at a prestigious law firm, earned a generous salary, and owned a pristine home with his pregnant wife. She did needlepoint and decorated pillows as a hobby. She even sold the pillows for a modest income. Harold was very proud of her. On the contrary, Morty was not proud of me, and he could not compete with his roommate's stellar success.

We all went to a restaurant in Philadelphia, where we met up with two female friends Morty and Harold knew during college. The women were lobbyists in Washington, D.C., and opinionated. They dominated the dinner conversation.

I sat next to Harold and quietly conversed with him. I told him about the awkward positioning of the toilet in the stair landing in a Paris inn where I once stayed. I could not contribute to the conversation with the lobbyists. I was desperate for words and felt I was choosing an overly personal topic to discuss with Harold. The lobbyists probably didn't have boyfriends. They were strong-willed and eyed me with daggers from across the table. They had most likely never encountered a female architect. I wasn't knowledgeable about politics, current events, or bestselling books, so I struggled to converse with these women whose enthusiasm for their jobs had no limits. They certainly weren't going to address the architecture in Washington, D.C.

I wasn't prepared for this situation. I felt excluded and fell into my pit of despair, turning inward. We left the restaurant, and I continued to walk alone in front of the group. Morty did little to comfort me.

While Morty and I were in the train station waiting to go back to New York, he ordered me to stand by our luggage while he purchased our return tickets. I felt sweaty and conspicuous, disconnected from reality. Morty seemed unsure of how to cope with my unattractive and unstable behavior. He treated me as an object of failure, and I was sure it was because he didn't love me. He tolerated me and was anxious not to create a scene. After we boarded the train, Morty told me I could have held my own with the two lobbyists because I was an architect. But I failed in my conversation with them, and my confidence for a bright future was shattered.

My exterior world was promising. I lived in a beautiful apartment, acquired architectural jobs, had a boyfriend, and my parents lived nearby. In contrast, my inner world was in turmoil and lacked direction. I had a silent, invisible illness that was expanding, and it was crippling me from moving forward in my life.

I decided to go home for a while. Morty was silent and didn't inform my parents about my unstable behavior. But my symptoms of being withdrawn, failing to sleep, and wanting to run away repeated in episode after episode, and my fears of isolation became more severe. And Dad could tell by my glassy eyes when I was melting down. I wanted to run away from my disturbing, punitive thoughts and go across America to California, the promised land, and find Robert Redford and marry him, commencing a new life.

Dad used all his strength to keep me from running away. He feared I would never be found and that I would end up homeless. He summoned the police and an ambulance. They immediately arrived at the house and threatened to place me in a straightjacket if I didn't comply and submit to being hospitalized.

An ambulance transported me to the county hospital. A few days later, I transferred to the private hospital. I repeated the same familiar routine, and in a few weeks, the doctor released me. I was discovering that each time I climbed out of my delirium, my inner voice became more reasonable. The effects of the angel dust seemed to be wearing off; however, my episodes were becoming more dangerous and life threatening.

CHAPTER 19

I deserted my job in downtown Manhattan and remained unemployed for a short period of time while I contemplated my next career move. I was hell-bent on finding a designer position despite my lack of experience. It was unrealistic. Regardless of all my meltdowns, Morty persisted in living with me. Ours was a loveless, symbiotic relationship where he got the lion's share of benefits, but I got to appease my loneliness.

When I started sliding into my fears of the future, Morty often quoted President Franklin Roosevelt: "The only thing we have to fear is fear itself." Morty believed he was comforting me and rationalizing what I was feeling. This worked briefly, but my fears always returned and resonated strongly in my gut, impossible to eliminate.

Morty showed me a list he had created for the sake of my improvement. On the list he wrote that I should fix my teeth and my nose, place dishes in the dishwasher without leftover food particles on them, and so forth. He claimed if I addressed these issues, then my social life would improve. What social life? Was he planning on dumping me on another man? This list was one more thing feeding into my poor self-image, and I couldn't even admonish him for his insensitive tirade because he was earnest about trying to help me. I was sad and believed I was not good enough because Morty didn't find me attractive and picked me apart little by little. I knew he didn't cherish me, but he remained a stable force in my life and kept an eye out for my reoccurring episodes.

About this time, in the fall of 1982, Dad and Dr. Samuels sought a specialist who had extensive knowledge of medicines used to treat mental disorders. His clinical experience would enable him to accurately diagnose my breakdowns and determine how my mental disorder should be addressed. So they vehemently urged me to have a session with this specialist. I reluctantly visited his office, which was located at a major hospital in Manhattan. I made this journey alone because I insisted I would independently work to resolve my serious mental condition. I filled out several forms, leaving great chunks of description blank, since only Dad was qualified to answer them. Therefore, the doctor had only a little information about my episodes to use in his analysis of my situation.

The doctor and I engaged during a brief session, and he diagnosed me with manic-depressive disorder (now known as bipolar disorder). My experiences of going days without sleep and having super energy were the manic side. The depressive side caused my feelings of inadequacy and abandonment with no hope for a future. In his evaluation, the doctor didn't consider my psychosis, my illusory world where I imagined revolutions and persecution, or my feelings of being a pariah and an object of scrutiny. The diagnosis didn't address my condition fully because I was too brief in my description of my symptoms, and the doctor should have consulted with Dr. Samuels and my father.

The doctor prescribed a daily dose of Lithium. This was difficult for me because I was careless in establishing and sticking to a medication regimen. Taking lithium required me to have blood tests every three months to regulate and monitor the level in my bloodstream. I didn't believe the lithium was effective, so I stopped taking it after three months. That was the end of my medicinal exploration. I kept taking Thorazine in challenging times.

Meanwhile, Jack, my vagabond boyfriend from my college days, got in touch with me while visiting his grandmother in Manhattan. He lived in South Africa and worked in an established architectural firm in Johannesburg. I had a secret date with him and told Morty I was meeting a girlfriend in Manhattan. I wore a new outfit just for Jack so I would look beautiful. He had shaved his beard and mustache and no longer looked Bohemian. His family was still scattered. His mother lived in Paris, his father in Belgium, his older brother in South Africa, and his younger brother in Chicago. Like Jack, my brother was stationed all over the world as an officer in the military. I rarely had the opportunity to see my brother, but we spoke on the phone several times a year. He had attended military college and then entered the service.

Jack and I held hands, but he asked me why I seemed tentative. I informed him that in his absence, I had continued with my life and was seriously dating another man. Jack and I were star-crossed lovers. He thought I would wait for him as he pursued his life in South Africa, which was unlikely, unreasonable, and unrealistic. I was elated to be with Jack and enthralled to learn he still thought of me after all this time since we dated in the spring of 1977. If only he had remained in Manhattan and made a life near me. We ate dinner together and strolled the streets of Manhattan. Then I returned to the doldrums of my apartment and Morty.

I was still job hunting. Dad introduced me to a construction project manager who had connections to an established architectural firm in Manhattan. This gentleman pleaded with me not to take a job at the firm. Instead, he urged me to work in the construction company where he was employed. He insisted that he be my mentor and that the work would be much more lucrative and steadier. I was stubborn, though, and clung to my aspirations of being a designer in a plush office while tending to affluent clients. I wasn't interested in being at an unkempt office at a construction site. Finally, the gentleman caved and got me a job as a draftsman in the renowned architectural firm. I was hired right before Christmas 1982. It was a mundane job, and my salary was minimal. I worked on the construction site of a warehouse being converted into an office building. I desperately wanted to be working in their Fifth Avenue office instead.

Commuting included traveling on the train, taking a subway, and walking a stretch to reach the east side of Manhattan on 47th Street. I devotedly commuted in all weather conditions because I was determined to establish a good reputation. When I started the job, the company gave me a Christmas bonus, which I genuinely appreciated. I was off to a good start.

The on-site office on the second floor was split into two sections: the construction management team and the architectural drafting team. The head draftsman was a slim, quiet gentleman who sat across from my work station. Sara, a fellow draftsman, sat directly in front of me. She was petite and sported a short, blonde hairdo. Sara was articulate and a stellar draftsman. Even though she was younger than me, she was already married to her college boyfriend, who was a doctor. Sara exemplified my aspirations. She had it all, and I believed I had nothing. Morty never alluded to getting married, especially after witnessing my breakdowns. I failed at finding a caring, accepting, and sensitive partner. Instead, I accepted being used for intimacy, housing, and money. I was too passive and insecure to end the relationship with Morty. Everyone's situation seemed better than mine.

Sara had been employed by the firm long before I was hired. Since she was an excellent draftsman, she received all the juicy tasks, such as drafting wall details, door details, layouts of interior spaces, and more. Her drawings were precise and beautiful. Each was a practical model for me to emulate.

I informed the chief draftsman that I yearned for challenging tasks, and eventually, he assigned me the fireplace design for the conference room in the converted building. I struggled with the design. I used a reference book called *Architectural Graphic Standards* to establish the dimensions of the opening. I made a critical error in making the height of the hearth too high in proportion to the width, and it was obvious after construction. I was extremely embarrassed, but luckily, the chief draftsman defended me instead of being irate.

I often ate lunch with Sara and another draftsman, Dana, who sat behind me. Dana was engaged to David, an associate of the firm at the Fifth Avenue office. She also was petite and had curly black hair and olive skin. Dana was a talented draftsman and had been with the company for more than a year. I felt left out knowing that everyone had somebody who cared about them except me.

In the spring of 1983, I experienced a minor meltdown. I was absent from my job for two weeks. I imagined that my fellow workers looked down on me since I was a poor draftsman and unsuccessful at designing the fireplace. I couldn't return to a place where I was regarded as an incompetent fool and the lowest paid draftsman. Both my mind and the reality of my life had me convinced that I wasn't good enough. I stayed in my apartment, sinking into a black hole of depression, anxiety, and my misguided perceptions of being an outcast. I attempted to sleep away my hellish existence, and in a brief amount of time, I managed to get better. I acknowledged that my success avoided admission to a psych ward, which was becoming all too familiar to me.

When I returned to work, determined to do my best after this minor meltdown, I walked a fine line between my warped reality and a poor reputation. I guarded everything I said for fear I would accidentally reveal my secret mental disorder to my coworkers and boss. I imagined they were judging me and considered me peculiar. I didn't know how to move forward and be objective in problem-solving. My symptoms of imagining an isolated existence were slowly becoming a self-fulfilling prophecy.

Day in and day out, I attended work and floundered in the mundane tasks assigned to me. Every morning, I purchased a cup of coffee and a blueberry muffin to eat at the office. This was the highlight of my day and a diversion from my lonely existence.

CHAPTER 20

During work hours, Dana overtly made plans for her wedding. She and David were overjoyed about the upcoming ceremony. She discussed her reception and floral arrangements, and she sent invitations to her close circle of contacts. I was privy to it all because she sat right behind me. She did not invite me to her wedding since I was a relatively new employee. Even though this made sense, I felt left out. It seemed only right that she would invite me too. Half of the firm's employees were invited.

She spoke at length about her wedding details to Sara and me during our lunches, which was the reason I stopped having lunch with them. I felt like the third wheel. Instead, I spent my lunch hour shopping for attractive clothes. I discovered immense peace and tranquility through my retail therapy. Luckily, Dad was giving me a monthly allowance in addition to my salary. I contributed this stipend to the joint account I shared with Morty. Slowly, we began to save a reasonable amount of money.

One day, the owner of the firm came to observe all his employees at work. He perched at Sara's desk and glanced at me with a disdainful expression. Everyone but me gathered around the boss as he reviewed Sara's impressive drawings and praised her. I sank into my seat, feeling inferior and insignificant.

The boss then barked at me to pass him the phone near my desk. I sat completely still. I didn't deserve his blatant disrespect, and I defied his commands. Everyone else was in awe of his presence and felt honored by his attention. Finally, another draftsman broke the tension when he reached over and handed the boss the phone. The owner kept looking at me with disapproval. I had fought his arrogance with insolence, and everyone had witnessed it. Work was never quite the same after that.

Caren, my best friend from high school, invited Morty and me to her wedding in the summer of 1983. I had befriended her in our sophomore year and steadily garnered a friendship that lasted. In our junior year, we went to a ring-bearing ceremony and party weekend at my brother's military college. Both of us got terribly drunk, and my brother admonished me for putting us in a careless and dangerous situation. Then, in the beginning of my senior year, I came down with mononucleosis and was absent from school for three weeks. Caren tutored me in math, and when I returned to class, I aced an exam because she patiently taught me the complex subject in its simplest terms.

Caren met Andrew at college. She was Armenian and Christian, and he was Jewish, so they agreed to be married by a justice of the peace at an elegant catering hall near our hometown.

Morty and I sat with Caren's family, which included her happily married older sister and two younger sisters. I was happy for Caren but again felt convinced I would be alone for the rest of my life. I felt even worse when Morty declined to be in a photo taken of Caren with her family and friends. Morty obviously didn't have any plans of including me in his future, and I was too compromised to end our relationship.

The night of their wedding was balmy. Andrew's family came from California and held a champagne toast to usher in the union of the well-established families. Caren and Andrew were graduates from America's top colleges and had obtained doctoral degrees in biology and chemistry. They were a powerhouse couple. Although I felt inferior, I was not jealous, nor did I pity myself. I just kept moving forward like a tank in battle. It was Caren's time to be married and to experience success since she spent most of her youth carefully planning and studying how to be a respected scientist. She never knew about my struggles, and I never offered to share them with her.

During that summer, Morty and I took a trip to Florida to visit his parents and, briefly, my maternal grandparents, who lived near one another. Morty's parents lived in a condo surrounded by a golf course in a gated community. They were serious golfers and spent many days in retired bliss playing on the beautiful grounds.

Morty's mother decorated her entire living space in a soothing peach color. His parents were reserved at first, and I suspected Morty had informed them of my mental strife. I felt like they struggled to be polite and did not approve of me dating their son. That fueled my feelings of loneliness and inadequacy. Morty and I stayed at their condo, and I slept in their den on a pullout couch. Perhaps his parents were suspicious or disappointed because Morty hadn't introduced us earlier. We had been a couple for a year. Maybe they sensed Morty's lack of enthusiasm and affection for me and our relationship.

My grandparents lived nearby in a gated community that had a pool and clubhouse. The community consisted of one-story clusters and a lagoon running through the backyards. I had exactly one day to visit my grandparents while Morty visited his college roomate's parents. Morty took his time preparing that day. He didn't care that I wanted to spend a substantial amount of time with my grandparents. Instead, he looked at the visit as a burden and chore, something he was in no rush to get to.

My grandparents met Morty briefly and didn't like him. How they saw right through him baffled me, but I was obstinate about following their advice to get rid of him and find someone more genuine.

My grandmother decorated her condo with lustrous green overtones. Green was her favorite color, and she made it known. She was a beautiful woman who aged well. She showed very few wrinkles and had big, brown eyes that dominated her stunning facial features. She always wore a wig because she had damaged her hair by dyeing it in her youth. She smoked cigarettes, and my grandfather smoked cigars. They religiously had a shot of whiskey every day. My grandfather loved to fish in the sea, which was the main reason they relocated to Florida from Brooklyn.

My grandmother had one good friend who moved to the same community. She didn't have any other friends because she was critical of people, and without realizing it, she sabotaged many potential friendships with her sharp tongue.

My grandmother had very little emotional or familial support after her mother died when she was thirteen years old. Her unchecked critical ways inhibited my mother from pursuing a career in one of her many talents: singing, playing the violin, and designing women's fashion. Between the conventions of the time and my grandmother's critical nature, my mother did not persist. My mother was then critical of me. Criticism was passed from one generation to the next.

My mother inherited many of her talents from my grandfather, who was a self-taught electrician. He lit up all of Chinatown in Manhattan. When his business partner extorted money from the company, that was the end of my grandfather's enterprising business. He never recovered from his financial downfall and became a building superintendent instead.

My grandfather was the youngest in his family. His father was from northern Russia and played the flute in an orchestra. In the late 1800s, many European musicians immigrated to America via the sponsorship of John Philip Sousa. Once here, they performed in his famous band. My great-grandfather did just that and joined the band as a skilled flutist. The band traveled a lot, and sometimes my great-grandfather was away from his family for two months at a time.

While my great-grandfather was gone, my great-grandmother slept all the time. As a result of his dysfunctional family, my grandfather was both reserved and pensive. His half sister, Bessy, a gorgeous woman who eventually owned a thrift store on Second Avenue in Manhattan, practically raised him.

Unfortunately, my grandfather did not have the opportunity to bond with either of his parents. Then, as the target of my grandmother's criticism, he was unable to nurture my mother, their only child.

My grandparents comforted me with their warm welcome. Morty went on his way to visit Harold's parents so I had a few sacred hours with my grandparents. I was so fatigued that I asked my grandmother if I could rest on one of her twin beds. As soon as my body hit the sheets, I fell into a deep sleep and the land of dreams. When I woke up after an hour, I felt refreshed and spent a little time with my grandparents in their green living room.

Morty returned, and I found myself wishing I had heeded their advice. I should have stayed with my grandparents instead. I should have severed my ties with Morty and his cold family, but I lacked the gumption to act on my best interests and instincts.

We returned to join Morty's parents for dinner. His mother prepared deli sandwiches that were not New York quality and tasted like bad meat to me. Everyone ate jovially, but after an hour of unpleasantness, I felt weak and vomited. I had to retire early. Morty did not realize that I had a severely upset stomach. He thought I was just being dramatic. He was upset I had spoiled a perfectly good evening.

CHAPTER 21

After a few more days in Florida, we returned to New York. The apathetic and uncaring vibes I felt from Morty and my lack of success in my work environment became intertwined and manifested in lower self-esteem. I was unable to climb out of the murky waters of my sullen existence. I was not using my creative abilities, and I felt like I was trapped in a dead-end job again. Day in and day out, I trudged along without passion or personal growth. I was deeply frustrated and didn't know how to realize my trapped potential. I was alone, immersed in my lonely struggle, with no direction, goal, or understanding of how to find help in establishing myself in my profession. I had no mentor to look out for my best interests. I was settling in my discouraging existence, without the courage to challenge my misguided direction, and succumbing to a shallow path toward self-destruction. Only my unchanneled ambition kept me going.

The winter of 1983 arrived, cold as ever. One weekend, Morty and I were driving to our favorite hamburger joint as snow fell gently outside. Visibility was compromised, and a car skidded at a traffic light and hit us. The front end of my car was dented. Morty wasn't injured, but when the ambulance arrived, he insisted that he be taken to the emergency room to be examined. He displayed no concern whatsoever for me. I could tell from their demeanor that the ambulance technicians had noticed the awkward relationship between Morty and me. As if his neglect and apathy weren't enough to make me feel bad, he blamed the accident on my driving. This incident affected me deeply, and I continued to feel like the object of Morty's scrutiny.

Christmas approached, and Morty was preparing to visit his parents in Florida. As Morty planned his trip, my fears of loneliness and despair weighed heavily on me. I was afraid to sleep at night because I feared that when I woke up, I would find myself abandoned. Everyone else would have left Earth in spaceships. An anxiety and mania more powerful than any dream began to take over.

The firm I worked for had a huge Christmas party. I couldn't attend because I hadn't slept in several nights. I was delirious. I believed everyone was conspiring against me. I continued to lose sleep. I became trapped in my apartment, pacing back and forth while contemplating an escape from my tormented world. Where could I go to find solace and start a new life? I had to run.

On Christmas Eve 1983, Morty was leaving for Florida. He didn't know how to address my anguish, and he was eager to leave and pawn me off on someone else. He called my father and told him to come to the apartment. I continued to pace. I was a pariah and desperately alone in my meager attempts to survive an imagined war. My father arrived. I believed he was the enemy and that he was going to capture me and lock me up in a prison. Still, Morty abandoned me. He cared more about missing his flight than about me, and his cold indifference toward me should have been obvious to my father.

I mustered super strength as my delirium escalated, and I managed to get past my father. I frantically descended the fire-exit stairs to my rental car in the garage. My father swiftly followed me and tried to restrain me, but it was impossible. I drove to the entrance of the garage and nearly ran over my father when he attempted to block my exit. He was helpless. I drove aimlessly, then decided to head toward the John F. Kennedy Airport since I momentarily thought all Jewish people were embarking on a flight to Israel to escape an apocalyptic world. The airport was confusing to navigate, and I was unable to find an Israeli plane. I followed a road that led me to exit the airport, then I turned around and drove back into the airport while experiencing confusion and hopeless despair.

I finally exited the airport and drifted aimlessly. As I drove, I tossed my bag containing a photo of my brother parachuting when he was in the Eighty-Second Airborne Division of the US Army. I thought no one could identify me without my bag. I continued to drive until I reached a desolate road close to Jamaica Bay.

Meanwhile, my father alerted the police that I was missing and on a paranoid tirade. I finally parked the car on the side of the road, stepped out, and walked toward the water. I stopped walking just shy of the shoreline and stood frozen. My feet were submerged in snow, and I could hear the undulating waves resonating in my mind for hours until Christmas morning. The temperature was zero degrees, and the windchill factor was seventeen degrees below zero. In my manic state, I did not feel the cold or the numbness in my feet.

After a long time, I stepped into the shallow waters and slowly immersed myself. I looked toward the horizon and caught sight of a group of black sea creatures congregating in a circle beyond the shore. My fear of these creatures kept me from immersing myself completely. I slowly turned around and walked out of the water. My black down coat was as heavy as iron. Hours passed, and I stood motionless. I was numb to the failures in my life, to uncaring and loveless Morty, to the disconnected existence I endured, to my impending failures at my job, to the delusion that my family and everyone else abandoned me on Earth, and to the guilt over my sexuality, which lived deep within my gut. In the unforgiving cold, I was in solitude for a hopeless eternity.

CHAPTER 22

For some miraculous reason, as I stood outside freezing to death, my left hand felt warm, as if an imaginary being was embracing it and keeping it safe from the harmful cold. An angel protected me from dying in the arctic temperatures. The warmth of my hand was a harbinger of hope that one day a considerate, sincere man would discover and appreciate me, and I would not be alone.

As dawn arrived, I could see my rental car parked a short distance from where I stood. Luckily, a lady had seen me throw my bag out of the car, and she retrieved it. She reported it to the police, and they were able to find me when they discovered the rental car parked on the shoulder of the highway. The police scanned the area and found me as I was walking back to the car. The police officers approached me, undoubtedly concerned and astonished that I was outside all night in the extreme weather conditions. They embraced me delicately and guided me to their car. They asked me what my name was, and I replied with my standard fictitious name, Linda. They knew who I was though. Clearly, they surmised I was experiencing a mental breakdown of significant proportions.

I was barefoot, and my coat felt like a ton of bricks. They commented on my black feet and were surprised I could even walk. I was so deranged that I didn't feel any pain as my body began to thaw in the heated car. I sat quietly and allowed my fate to be determined by the genteel police officers.

They took me to the emergency room at Jamaica Hospital. The staff was concerned that I would develop pneumonia. They changed me out of my wet clothes and into a hospital gown. The nurses put me on a gurney in the hallway since the emergency room was cramped with patients.

My father finally arrived at the hospital and was apprehensive about my position in the hallway. He tried to contact Dr. Samuels and was desperate when the doctor didn't answer. After several hours, I was still stranded in the hallway and victim to the steady draft that passed through the doors. I didn't feel any pain since my limbs were still frozen and numb, but I was excruciatingly embarrassed about being nude under a short hospital gown. I was menstruating, and my blood was everywhere. My father decided to hire a private ambulance to transport me to the same private hospital as before. After several hours of waiting for an available bed in the psych ward of the private hospital, I was moved to a wheelchair and escorted to my room. I remained in a wheelchair for six weeks because my feet were badly injured from the freezing temperatures and snow.

I was admitted to the private hospital as Dr. Samuels' patient. The ward was oddly comforting since it was familiar to me, and it seemed my fate to end up there. My hospital room had two beds, but I was the only patient assigned to the room. I sat in the dark, reflecting on what had happened. I realized how fortunate I was, especially after learning about a man in New Jersey who stood in the snow overnight and had to have his feet amputated due to severe frostbite. And then I recalled the warm feeling on my left hand; the hand where, in marriage, a gold band symbolizing relentless commitment is worn. I clutched the belief that someone was out there waiting for me. It was too much to consider otherwise, with the harsh reality of sitting in the dark in a wheelchair on the psych ward.

A doctor startled me as he entered my room. He reminded me of a fellow student in the architecture program I attended in the North. In 1974, early in the first semester, the freshman architecture class had to perform a skit depicting the study of an assigned building in the vicinity of the college and neighboring towns. Our class of sixty students was divided into groups of six. My group was assigned to study the Greyhound bus terminal and perform the analysis of the building and surrounding context. We developed a skit that presented two students dressed up as suitcases relating the experiences and activities in a bus station. My group chose me and a student who looked like the doctor in my hospital room. The skit was so original and successful, the dean of the architecture program applauded and praised me. He jokingly told me I took up the wrong profession and instead should have pursued a career as an actress. I was a celebrity in the architecture program and never fully realized the impact of my performance.

In a procedure known as a blood gas test, the doctor drew blood from a major vein to check for a high white blood cell count. That would indicate I might have contracted pneumonia. I stopped him midway through because I could not tolerate the pain anymore. He asked me if I was hungry. I hadn't eaten in three days, but I was in too much pain to be hungry. The doctor informed me that he did not know the future of my blackened feet. I pondered the worst-case scenario. I felt like running, but I was fastened to the wheelchair, and my injured feet would not support me.

Dad visited in the evening and brought me toiletries and clothes. He was relieved that I was alive, but sadness dominated, and he was powerless to change the past.

Meanwhile, Morty was in Florida, and I didn't know if he had called my father to check on me or not. I don't remember Morty visiting me or if he went to my parents' home. He was on vacation in Florida for a long time, and his parents were probably relieved I was not there. Those people never experienced any mental illness, and they treated me as though I were inferior.

Dad was a rock of undying concern. Mom was a rock of nurturing love when she gathered the strength to be there. Mom and Dad never experienced anything like my episodic breakdowns, but they had to muster strength when they endured immense anxiety and fear.

Dad visited me in the psych ward much more than my mother. She couldn't handle the sight of me restricted to a wheelchair. In the end, she had no choice but to face my chronic illness since I was still in a wheelchair when I returned to their home to convalesce. The kind and diligent nurse in the psych ward taught me how to care for my bandaged feet. Twice daily, I changed the bandages and applied a topical antibiotic cream until the skin on my feet completely healed. Mom took me to the podiatrist numerous times, and gradually my ability to walk started to improve.

Mom and Dad hired a carpenter to build a ramp to the entrance of their house. I had my own bathroom, connected to the front bedroom, and that was where I changed my bandages. While I continued to recuperate at my parents' house, Morty continued to live in my apartment. Neither my parents nor I invited him over, so I did not see him often. Gradually, during the spring of 1984, I broke away from his uncaring, selfish motives.

CHAPTER 23

In February 1984, I returned to work, where I was happy to see Dana and Sara, but after two weeks, the manager fired me. I had just passed my one-year mark. I was shaken and deeply offended, but I didn't allow the situation to keep me from moving forward. I immediately sought a new position with an architecture firm in a building adjacent to my previous job. I asked the construction superintendent from my old job to recommend me for the new position. I was surprised and elated that the new super agreed to hire me as a draftsman. It was too hasty a decision, but I was optimistic about continuing my life despite my cyclical meltdowns. I had tons of ambition, which helped me transcend my mental strife, even though I didn't know how to direct my ambition or parlay it into a more successful career.

Finding my soul mate was the crux of my endeavors. I had more hope and enthusiasm about meeting Mr. Right than about climbing the corporate ladder. Still, I started my new job with gusto. My position, again, consisted of drafting miniscule assignments pertaining to the renovation of an interior office space. I quickly found myself on an endless loop of mundane tasks that did not engage my imagination or intellect. I befriended the drafters who sat next to me and fell into my old habit of conversing too much and working too little. Jack, the owner of the firm, told me that my drafting had to improve, or I would be terminated. I quickly became dissatisfied with my work since my assignments were so routine, meaningless, and boring, but I was able to move forward in my personal life.

I finally realized that I had to boot Morty out of my life and apartment. He was a hindrance in every way. When I broke the news, he was shocked and offended. But there was no yelling match or tears of remorse. The "cowardly lion" simply left with his tail between his legs. I forgot to collect my half of our savings, which amounted to three thousand dollars. Morty used the money to move to Florida, where he decided to live until he found his own place in New York. My mother and I placed his furniture in storage. I felt like I could finally create a beautiful living space without Morty and his ugly brown, corduroy chair. I broke free from the web of oppression and was available to pursue new relationships and endeavors.

Above the sofa in the living room, I hung cloth blueprints of The Commodore Hotel, which filled the wall space and created the illusion that the room was larger than it was. The blueprints came from the general superintendent at the hotel renovation job where I had worked. My living room was modern with a contemporary flair. It was cheerful and uplifting, a space I had yearned for all my life.

I stayed with Jack's company through the summer but quit in August. Then I secured a drafting position with an engineering firm that specialized in designing public roadways and parking lots. Before taking this job, I seriously considered how it would benefit me to work for a firm that differed from my previous positions. I started at the beginning of September, and the firm provided medical benefits after one month. The office was on the West Side of Manhattan, in the vicinity of Penn Station, so I didn't have to commute too far.

Socializing was paramount for me, since the ideal friend or Mr. Right could come along at any time. I was to draft a parking lot, which was tedious and boring. Instead, I took the opportunity to notice a handsome draftsman who sat a few rows behind me. I attempted to catch his attention, but he essentially ignored me. For the first time since I was employed anywhere, I remained a stranger to my coworkers. I began to focus more on my work than on seeking conversation.

Meanwhile, I remained friendly with Dana, even though she didn't invite me to her wedding, and I had been fired from the firm where we had worked together. She was still married to David. He was ten years older than Dana and had a son from a previous marriage. David's ex-wife made his financial situation challenging, but Dana was full of tolerance. They lived in a cozy townhouse in Greenwich Village, in Manhattan, and they were content.

Dana informed me that she and David were going to take a workshop similar to the popular Erhard Seminars Training of the 1970s, where a group of strangers participated in mental exercises that would empower them to cope with emotional burdens and become more assertive about living life to the fullest. Dana and David invited me to participate in this special workshop. It seemed promising, and I thought I could vanquish my emotional demons and live life more peacefully if it worked. They also informed me that they wanted to introduce me to an available dentist who would be at the workshop.

The committee that organized the workshop mandated an interview with participants. The leader of the workshop, who did not have credentials in mental health, was absent during my interview. Instead, a dominating young woman and a conservative young man interviewed me. They were confident the program would help individuals lead a more fulfilling existence. My interview was successful, and I was accepted into the workshop. It commenced on a Wednesday and concluded on a Sunday, after five days of strenuous mental exercises.

I scheduled three vacation days to participate in this important workshop. I described the session to my amiable boss, and he kindly allowed me to take the time necessary to participate. Evidently my diligence toward my job impressed my boss, who genuinely liked me. He respected my work habits, which could not be said of my previous employers.

CHAPTER 24

One week before Halloween in 1984, the life improvement workshop convened at a YMCA in the heart of Manhattan. About twenty or thirty people from all walks of life participated. We each were given a notebook to record our troubles, self-analysis, and rambling thoughts. All of us mingled at first, but then we were divided into assigned groups and had to choose a buddy to work with throughout the duration of the workshop. I chose the dentist.

After we paired off, we engaged in mental exercises that were confrontational and anxiety-provoking. For example, one exercise took place in an imaginary lifeboat with space for only two survivors. Each group member had to publicly defend why they should not be left behind. I blurted out that I could survive and explained that I could endure the severe cold due to the subzero skiing days of my youth. I was immediately unsure of myself, which undermined my message. I was going to be left to perish in the ocean.

I was caught off guard by these exercises because the workshop interviewers led me to believe the workshop would consist of neutral lectures about expanding one's daily living and how to be assertive and capable. I cried and cried during one exercise. I couldn't control my emotions, and I began to break down. The dentist got into a physical altercation with another participant, which upset me and caused me to isolate myself from the group. My feelings of being an outcast resurfaced, and my partner, the dentist, was making a spectacle of himself.

The first session ended after dark, and it took me an hour to get back to my apartment. Since I was deeply agitated, I couldn't sleep, and my appetite vanished as well. My parents were on a five-day vacation that coincided with the workshop. I was on my own and struggled to keep my sanity. I reluctantly returned to the workshop on Thursday. The intense exercises brought out my demons, and I worked hard to conceal my history of mental illness. I was too afraid to drop the workshop altogether. Dana and David realized I was struggling to stay afloat, so they invited me to their home after the Thursday session. I declined since I was determined to run to my familiar apartment and stay there for eternity.

I contacted Dr. Samuels and asked him if I should return to the workshop on Friday. I described my immense fear and anxiety while participating in the stressful mental exercises. The doctor advised me not to return to the workshop and said he would see me Monday evening for our regular appointment. This meant I had to endure the weekend with my perilous imagination. He knew my parents were on vacation but didn't realize how deeply alone and isolated I was.

Although I spoke with the doctor, I remained frantic and was unable to sleep for another night. I did not return to the workshop on Friday. The organizers of the workshop attempted to coerce me to return. They antagonized me on the phone and fed into my paranoid emotions, but I meekly stood my ground and stayed in my apartment. The aggressive dentist came to my apartment and banged on my door while shouting and calling me a selfish bitch. I felt panicked, as if my privacy had been violated, but I did not open the door. He finally softened and left a letter under my door that I couldn't bring myself to read. I threw it in the garbage. I never found out if the words he wrote were angry or kind. I was frightened to leave my apartment in case the dentist lurked nearby. I waited until nighttime to drive to my parents' house, where I sought refuge.

Since I knew the code, I entered the house through the garage. Encountering the dark, empty house, I realized I would not find solace there, so I returned to my apartment. I hadn't slept for two nights, and my mind was separating from my body as I struggled to survive my anguish, both real and imagined. I felt like I was a pariah on an island in a chaotic sea, trapped with no signs of help on the horizon. I was stuck in quicksand. I decided to clean and organize my apartment. I prepared scrambled eggs for myself. Despite my lack of sleep, I overflowed with energy, a restless mania that kept me from sleeping. I stopped taking my daily dose of

Haldol, an antipsychotic I had become diligent in taking between episodes, when my life was normal and not spiraling into paranoia and illusory thoughts. While I cleaned my apartment, I stumbled upon a book about an American artist who lived in the nineteenth century. As I skimmed the book, I thought I could be a better artist but remembered how my confidence had been shattered in high school. The yearbook editors did not choose my illustration for the cover. Instead they selected the other art editor's design. I put up a fight to the end because my cover, simulating a peace sign and depicting a wreath of silhouettes portraying students in various school activities, was relevant to the times in 1974. The editors had the principal of the school fire me from my position as the coeditor of art. I was devastated, and being fired caused me to lose interest in pursuing a career as an artist. But leafing through my most cherished art book that day in my apartment briefly reignited my desire to be an artist. And I found some comfort in that.

Night came, and I tossed and turned again. Through my bedroom wall I could hear the piercing sounds of an electric drill and electric saw throughout the night. My neighbors were renovating their apartment. My paranoia took over, and delusions that the carpenter was going to persecute me with his relentless electric saw overwhelmed me. Saturday and Sunday bled into each other, and I clung to my art book, a symbol of comfort. Four nights passed, and I endured restless terror and no sleep. My parents phoned me on Sunday night when they returned from their vacation, and I did not indicate that I was falling apart. I did not want to be locked up for eternity. They suggested I pick up Ming Lee from the vet, where she was boarding, on Monday. I knew I could not care for Ming Lee, so I asked my parents to keep her for a few more days. Ming Lee was a comfort, but she would be in danger under my care. This I knew.

Sunday night passed with no sleep, and I finally saw Dr. Samuels Monday evening. We superficially discussed the workshop. On the surface, I appeared to be normal, but inside I was fraught with paranoid anxiety. I thought I was going to be killed. I was unkempt and had worn the same clothes for days, but the doctor did not seem to notice. Since I had not returned to the workshop and had worked through my anxiety without my parents, Dr. Samuels believed I was okay. He increased my dosage of Haldol and advised me to return on Thursday evening at our regular time. The doctor and my parents had minimal communication. My father couldn't do anything to keep my breakdown from escalating. The doctor had advised my parents to maintain a distance and let me work through my episodic distortions of reality alone. According to him, I would eventually return to normal.

After convening with the doctor Monday night, I returned to my apartment and desperately attempted to sleep. My neighbors continued to renovate their apartment, creating irritating noises that haunted me. Fear and terror consumed me. That was another night without sleep, and as the days and nights crawled onward, I was unable to distinguish one from the other.

I barged into Dr. Samuels' office Tuesday morning. He told me that it was not time for my appointment and that several of his patients were in crisis. He told me to come back at my appointed time on Thursday night. I hadn't slept for six days and six nights, and my anxiety and fears were as high as Mt. Everest. I was desperate for help, and I tried to communicate my dire situation to him. I failed to make my emergency known to the blindsided doctor. I was on a ship sinking to the bottom of the sea, where no one could hear my cries for help. My appearance was raggedy, and I wore my trench coat even though the sun shined outside. Meanwhile, I avoided my parents' phone calls and did not see them when they returned from their vacation Sunday. I feared they would commit me, and I would never be free again.

I finally informed Dad I would visit on Thursday. I was slowly going mad. Halloween arrived Wednesday. I hadn't slept for seven days and seven nights. Somehow, I managed to call the engineering firm and inform them that I was sick and would return in a few days. I reflected on the years I had been employed at numerous architecture firms. I was never promoted and was always delegated to the simplest of tasks. I was in the same position as when I started this circuitous journey ten years before, when I started the architecture program. I thought of letting go of architecture, and I began to consider fine art and its possibilities.

My mind raced back and forth. I berated myself harshly for my sexual history, believing I was a pariah because of my promiscuity, and I suffered the inability to pull out of my slow demise and lack of positive direction in my stagnant life.

I returned to my bed once again and heard only the noise coming from next door. It reminded me that I would be persecuted, crucified, destroyed—at any moment. I had to escape from this cruel world. And then I had a brilliant idea.

I gathered my flannel bedsheets and tied the ends together to form a long rope. I tied one end of the rope around my dining room table and climbed out of the window while gripping the sheet and attempting to rappel down the exterior wall. When I was in high school, I fell from a twelve-foot stone wall at the neighborhood beach and survived without injury. I felt I was invincible to any mishap. And I thought Dad would be proud of me for rappelling down a thirty-foot wall.

The pull of gravity was so strong I couldn't plant my feet against the wall to rappel. I screamed for help as my grip began to slip, and I instantly knew I was going to fall thirty feet. My neighbor heard my screams for help and called the police. No one could save me from falling though. I continued to scream and prayed I would survive my imminent fall. As I dangled from the window, I planned how I would fall. I went down feet first and then, on impact, I rolled to my right to protect my head from hitting the pavement and lessen the force on my feet and legs.

CHAPTER 25

Blackness enveloped me. When I awoke, I found myself in the ER of the private hospital. I lay on a gurney in a bewildered manic state, and I didn't feel any pain. I understood that I had survived a grave fall. The vertebrae of the lower lumbar section of my spine were shattered, and several nerves were dead. I had broken my back.

The ER staff wheeled me into another area, where the orthopedist attempted to determine the extent of my injuries. The doctor held a sharp pin and pricked different parts of my legs to see if I had any feeling or sensation. I didn't respond even though I could feel sensation in my legs. I was in shock. I could see my ankle bone protruding from the skin on my left leg. My right ankle was destroyed, and the doctor kept pricking me. Still no reaction. I couldn't respond. I didn't want to be there. I denied my condition. I was confused. The assisting doctor repeatedly reprimanded me for not responding.

In my sleepless mania, I believed I could be a superhero and survive anything. I soon realized I was a wounded soldier fighting to survive a personal war. We are all soldiers fighting to cope with daily life and to survive our fates. Every day is a battle, for we are soldiers of freedom, destiny, and choice. I chose to escape through a window, but I had not outrun the danger. The doctors planned immediate surgery to repair my back, and they were frustrated with my lack of response. It must have been four o'clock in the morning, and Dad was there with me. The hospital team then moved me into an MRI machine. Dad was crying, uncertain that I would ever walk again. Just before I entered the MRI machine, I asked the team of orthopedists, neurologists, and nurses if I would experience any pain. They reacted in unison by saying, "Not now!" The medical team acted swiftly and operated on me immediately after the MRI.

I woke up eight hours later and found myself in the ICU with an IV in my neck, casts on my legs that extended up to my hips, and a separate cast surrounding my torso. I couldn't move. I lay there feeling frantic. I was still in a manic state and was now fraught with discomfort. I couldn't run away.

I ripped out the IV. A nurse walked by and saw my bleeding neck. She placed pressure on my neck and then bandaged it. I was surprised she didn't try to reinsert the IV. Another nurse came to my room and took my vitals. She asked me what I did for a living. I replied that I worked as a draftsman in an architecture firm. She seemed impressed. No one asked me what led to my horrible accident, and they assumed I would never walk again. They were probably asking themselves, "How can a beautiful woman end up like this? What provoked her to fall thirty feet?"

Dad visited me in the ICU and brought a photograph of Ming Lee. It haunted me to think that my little dog was in the outside world while I was secluded in a cell. My mother could not cope with having a sick daughter who was suffering from an illness that only got worse with time. She didn't know what to do or how to help me.

Days and nights bled into one another. I sipped ice water and ate gelatin. Dad informed my brother of my tragedy, and Rob visited me about six weeks later, when he could take leave from the military.

I was still delusional and full of fear and anxiety. The doctors and nurses were going to kill me. I would be murdered in my bed. Or if not, I would wake up to a desolate world where every single human had left in spaceships, and I was left to perish. After three days in the ICU, my doctors moved me into the critical care unit. A transporter pushed my gurney through the hospital's hallways and into a cramped elevator filled with staff, patients, and visitors. When we reached my designated room, three nurses transferred me from the gurney to the bed. The room was bright white and offered no comforting decor. I was in the critical care unit for a month.

I had a roommate who slept most of the time. She had had her gallbladder removed, which was a significant surgical procedure at the time. Dad hired aides to keep me company and comfort me since I was restricted to my bed and still too delirious to sleep peacefully. The Jamaican aides were warm and compassionate. They never asked me how I became an invalid, but at a time when I was afraid to close my eyes, it was nice to have them there. I endured several weeks with broken sleep, sweat-inducing anxiety, and crippling fear.

I had a urinary catheter that led to a plastic bag where the urine was collected. I had to drink plenty of fluids to prevent the catheter from clogging and blocking the flow of urine. I couldn't feel the catheter because the nerves in my lower back that controlled the bladder and colon were dead. Nerves do not regenerate; therefore, I remain incontinent.

Early one morning, Dr. Morris, the orthopedist who operated on me, entered my room and began pricking my exposed toes to check if I had any sensation. This time I responded that I felt the pin. The doctor believed I would not walk again. His opinion derived from the large operation I underwent and the extent of the nerve damage, which was still unknown. He didn't want to give me false hope. The surgical team took a bone graft from my hip and fused the bone into my lumbar region to rebuild my shattered vertebrae. The doctor placed a steel rod next to the fused spine to serve as a rigid support. Dr. Morris rebuilt my right ankle with steel pins and plates during a four-hour surgery. When I wanted to turn to my side in the hospital bed, I had to stiffly move my entire body so as not to disturb my newly fused spine.

I turned often after my paranoia slowly subsided. The radiator in my room did not work properly, so I sweltered under the oppressive heat and the casts that covered two thirds of my body. There was no relief, so I sipped chilled soda and sucked on ice cubes to survive my tortuous circumstances. The doctors increased my Haldol. Whether the medication or time plus sleep healed my mind, I do not know, but I finally reached the threshold to peace. My distraught mother made the effort to visit me, and she brought me an old toothbrush from home. The heat made me cranky beyond belief, and I lashed out at her for not bringing me a new one instead. She appeared stoic, and I found it difficult to communicate with her. My mother's love and anguish were buried under a mountain of stress. Her expression seemed hard. I couldn't understand her at the time. I felt neglected but failed to realize that my mother was sandwiched between her ailing neurotic parents, my brother parachuting in the army, and my crippling illness. She brought me one large, white flower, and I embraced its beauty and delightful smell. The flower camouflaged my mother's indifferent suffering. She was incapable of both nurturing me and protecting herself from the broken daughter she witnessed before her. All the dreams she once had for me were lost, and her silent disappointment plagued my soul.

I yearned to curl my legs and sleep in a fetal position. Having to lie straight and rigid in a room that was beginning to mimic the climate of hell was intolerable. I wasn't interested in daytime television, and I could not concentrate enough to escape into a book, so I conversed a little with the aides. My roommate had recovered and left the hospital. As time passed, my leg casts were cut from my hips to my knees, allowing me some relief as I recovered. I started communicating with my friends again, and Dana and David visited me. They struggled to hide their reactions, and I could tell they were stunned by the extent of my injuries. They brought a box of bakery cookies, which we shared while we struggled to converse. They didn't pry. I assumed they thought I tried to commit suicide by jumping out of my window. I don't think they understood my epic paranoia, delusions of being murdered and abandoned, and low self-esteem that undermined the core of my relationships. They were sympathetic though, and I appreciated the contact with the outside world. I did not feel connected to anyone but felt the strong need for human contact to cope with my serious injuries. My future was a question mark.

Somehow Morty learned about my accident. Perhaps Dad informed him. Morty showed up at the hospital to visit, and I complained that I was desperately bored. He advised me to use the time to break the bad habit of biting my fingernails. Insensitive and tacky as usual, his cruel criticism pierced my lonely heart. He could have offered to purchase several magazines from the hospital gift shop or a cuddly teddy bear, both signs of sensitive affection. No, the bastard was incapable of such sweet ideas. Morty left, and it was as though he had never visited. I was glad that I had rid myself of this uncaring, insensitive opportunist.

Mom visited me in the afternoons, and Dad came to the hospital at night. Although they were relentless in their care for me, I carried a gnawing feeling of abandonment since I knew Dr. Samuels couldn't care less. He was on vacation during my first week in the hospital. As usual, Dad tried to communicate with him, and he finally got through when the doctor returned. I guess Dr. Samuels figured that my problems and I weren't going anywhere, and he could address them when he returned from his vacation.

Before my leg casts were shortened, Dr. Samuels finally came to visit me in the hospital. I could tell by his reaction that he was stunned to see my injured body, but he quickly composed himself to minimize the gravity of a situation that evolved in his negligent absence. I complained to him about my lonely existence. The doctor told me I should consider the glass half-full. After all, I had a job in an acclaimed field, I resided in a beautiful apartment, and I had a boyfriend. Dr. Samuels didn't realize or remember that I had severed my relationship with Morty. The doctor never mentioned my parents, who formed the backbone of my recovery. They were always there for me.

Mom and Dad were at a loss as to how to address my worsening illness, so they kept blindly summoning Dr. Samuels to treat me. He relished the money we paid, but he failed to seek out a psychiatrist who treated high-risk patients like me.

At the end of my second week in the hospital, part of the medical team measured me for a plastic, torso brace I had to wear full-time for nine months. The brace supported my back and kept it upright as my fused spine healed.

Luckily, health insurance paid for my surgery and the torso brace, which totaled more than $16,000. If I had been working at the engineering firm for less than a month, I wouldn't have qualified for the health insurance.

My hospital room continued to be unbearably hot, and my indwelling catheter got clogged. I screamed from the pain of my full bladder, but the nurses were waiting for the resident doctor, who was out on break. Finally, after I suffered dire pain, they cleaned the catheter so I could urinate.

Three-and-a-half weeks passed in the critical care unit, and then the moment arrived for me to sit upright. I experienced excruciating pain as I slowly moved my body to an upright position. I suffered enough pain for ten people. The nurse brought a wheelchair to my bedside. The immense pain surprised me since the only agony so far had been the constricting casts and the IV in my arm for two weeks.

I was finally out of my hospital room! I moved my wheelchair into the hallway and greeted every person I saw. I still had casts on both legs below my knees and a torso brace, but at least I was mobile in my wheelchair. Little by little, hope surfaced from a dark cave. I was able to sleep, eat, and feel content.

After one month in the private hospital, I moved to a rehab facility in New York City. My father asked Morty to ride with me in the ambulance. Morty was reluctant, but he eventually consented to my father's wishes. That was the least he could do.

CHAPTER 26

Morty hastily left my side as soon as we arrived at the rehab facility. An amiable nurse greeted me and guided me to the second floor of the bustling facility. I shared a room with three other patients. In the bed next to mine was an African American woman who was about fifty-five years old. Her name was Evelyn. She was recovering from a stroke, and her right leg was dysfunctional, so she was undergoing intensive physical therapy.

Before I could settle into my new surroundings, Dr. O'Hara came to welcome me. He gently demanded I be honest about my fall. Since the doctor was charming and trustworthy, I told him the truth—I climbed out of my apartment window and fell thirty feet. I felt self-conscious about my wounds and realized I made a mistake by revealing the truth to the handsome doctor. I was immediately drawn to him and his bedside manner. I was proud that I survived such an accident, but I remained slightly embarrassed about how the fall came about.

Dr. O'Hara was young, unmarried, and dedicated to his patients and profession. My pipe dreams included dating him after I healed entirely.

Dr. O'Hara would never be interested in pursuing someone like me. I was full of scars and imperfections, and I was afflicted with a mental disorder. Still, I fantasized about creating a life with him. I should have told him I fell off a ladder. My dream of being a couple with the earnest doctor helped me survive and cope with the healing process. I forged ahead with my recovery and was hopeful he would respond to my romantic vibes.

I was at the rehabilitation facility for only one day before two female relatives from my father's side of the family visited me. They arrived uninvited with the sole purpose of gawking at me. They gossiped with each other about me. Each relative visited separately for about five minutes instead of politely visiting me together.

I didn't realize their curious agenda, but when the second relative walked in, Evelyn blurted, "Is that the same relative I just saw?"

The relatives looked similiar and had intentionally dressed alike to confuse me, and Evelyn caught on to their intentions. They chuckled, undoubtedly feeling less alone in their own familial misery on account of my downfall.

Every day, I participated in a schedule of activities. In the afternoon, I took the elevator to the seventh floor in my wheelchair, which I would use for the next six months. I believed I would walk again, counter to the doctor's assumptions. It was just a matter of my bones healing for the next six months. On the seventh floor, there was a physical therapy area with weight machines and an elevated floor mat. I used the weight-bearing machines to strengthen my arms, and I transferred myself from my wheelchair to the elevated mats. I stretched my legs as I worked out with a certified physical therapist every day.

The seventh floor was the hub for all the rehab patients: victims of strokes, accidents, crimes, and sports injuries. Physical therapy helped us to eventually lead an independent life while adapting to our physical limitations. I met a famous polo player from Argentina who was trampled by horses and suffered brain damage. He always managed to say hello to me even though he struggled to get the words out. His mother, who sat by his side, agonized about her son's tragedy. I felt moved by my fellow patients' plights. As I learned more about their situations, I slowly realized I was not the only human suffering or adapting to an unfortunate circumstance. I was fortunate I did not land on my head. I would have died if I had not planned how to fall. I wasn't paralyzed like so many rehab patients I encountered. All of the patients on the seventh floor accepted their fate and moved ahead.

In the mornings, I visited the greenhouse on the first floor of the center. An enormous cockatoo greeted me from the perch in its cage and constantly asked, "How are you?" The daily interactions with this bird amused me and made me happy.

My roommates didn't get to have the adventures I did. The young woman across from my bed suffered from scleroderma, a severe tightening of the skin that eventually envelopes the entire body. Every day, she was submerged in a bath to relieve the pain. Despite her condition, she maintained a positive attitude and was grateful that her devoted boyfriend visited daily. He was kind and caring. Another roommate was an elderly lady who suffered a major stroke and remained in a semicoma. Eventually, she was relocated to another critical care unit.

Mom and Dad visited me on the weekends. I frequently took them to the gift shop on the first floor near the greenhouse. They didn't share my enthusiasm for shopping, but I insisted on purchasing a maroon wallet and a quilted cosmetic bag to lift my spirits. And they finally went along with my retail therapy. When I returned to my room, I placed my cosmetics into the attractive, new bag and discarded my used one. Evelyn immediately salvaged it from the garbage can by our beds, and I felt guilty that I had not offered it to her. I said, "Evelyn, I would have gladly given you my bag. I am so sorry I didn't think of you."

She was extremely grateful, and when her minister came to visit, he blessed me for my kindness. I always gave Evelyn my baked potato during dinner. She informed my parents many times, "She don't eat her baked potato!" Evelyn was endearing, and Mom and Dad chuckled about the fate of my baked potatoes. My spirits improved as our friendship grew.

One of the female aides was from South Africa. She had dark skin and taunted Evelyn, whose skin was lighter. The aide was jealous of Evelyn's appearance, and she lashed out by telling her, "You've been nowhere in this world." Evelyn adamantly responded, "I have been everywhere through the books I have read!" Evelyn defended her dignity when the resentful and angry aide challenged and insulted her. We were at the mercy of this aide because she maintained our hygiene by cleaning our bodily eliminations, a job that was undignified but essential. I hated being stranded in my bed and unable to stand up, both physically and metaphorically, for Evelyn. The aide was uncontrollably vile to Evelyn, but we stuck together during those harsh times. We were relieved when the offensive aide left and other aides tended to us for the duration of our stay.

After a few days at the rehab facility, a nurse removed my indwelling catheter. Every six hours, the nurse catheterized me, since I no longer had a plastic bag to collect my urine. I was extremely dismayed by my inability to urinate normally, a severe consequence of the accident. The doctors were still uncertain I would walk again, but I was hopeful and determined. One of the nurses taught me how to administer the catheter myself. Dr. O'Hara assured me that it would be easy to carry a fourteen-inch catheter in my tote, and as time moved forward, it was.

I treated anything Dr. O'Hara said like pearls of wisdom. I always clamored for his attention even though he acknowledged me only briefly. I obsessed over Dr. O'Hara, and Evelyn knew my affections could never be requited. I was just one patient of many in his busy regime. I was extremely disappointed when he was reassigned to a different floor.

One day my brother, who was living near an army base in Colorado, visited me. I was overjoyed to see him. He brought an amusing board game that we played together.

When my phone rang, my brother swiftly answered it with, "Gino's Pizzeria." It was Dr. Samuels, calling for the first time since I moved to rehab. I was curt with him and ended the conversation abruptly. By this point, Dad and I were considering a lawsuit against Dr. Samuels. Dad's college roommate was an eminent lawyer we summoned for the potential case. For the seven years I had been Dr. Samuel's patient, my meltdowns became more and more life-threatening. It was blatantly obvious he was unable to treat me and should have assigned a doctor who was more capable of treating high-risk patients.

At the rehab center, my parents and I convened with a chief psychiatrist, Dr. Chu. He was taken aback when I explained why I was in a wheelchair. He said, "Life is a one-act play, and one must proceed with caution and conservative measures." He was deeply concerned about my future, and he referred me to a prominent psychiatrist in Long Island. That referral was a new beginning filled with promise.

CHAPTER 27

After the eye-opening session with Dr. Chu, I returned to my room, and my parents went home. As I prepared for bed, I pondered Dr. Chu's words. I assumed life was a three-act play consisting of a beginning, middle, and end. I ruminated over Dr. Chu's adamancy. Dr. Samuels never insisted I be cautious in my endeavors. Dr. Chu's words stuck like superglue.

I contacted Reva, an old friend from my camp days who lived in the same town as my co-op apartment. She was pleased to hear from me, and she and her husband visited me at the rehab center one evening. I felt remorseful that I could not attend her recent wedding. Her husband was an engineer who emigrated from Russia with his brother and parents. Reva's husband spoke with a distinguished Russian accent and used his math skills on Wall Street. He was immersed in the stock market. Reva was fortunate to have consistency in her life as well as security, devotion, and direction. I was perpetually stranded in the wilderness of singledom.

I had my sights set on Dr. O'Hara despite my inner, gnawing feeling that he was beyond my reach and that I wasn't good enough. I habitually pursued impossible opportunities and ran after the wrong men—those who were unavailable and selfish, who didn't understand and appreciate me, who thought I was awkward, or who had a hidden dark side. I was safeguarding my own secrets. My friends probably wondered what happened to me during my break. Those who visited me at the rehab hospital got an eyeful of my injuries, but they always maintained a façade of being content to see me. No one dared comment or ask about my physical situation.

Yvonne from my college days and Dana from work, visited me during the evenings, which made my days and nights tolerable. I appreciated having contact with the outside world, even if it was a world that was progressing without me, while I regained my strength and composure and survived without much purpose.

One evening in December 1984, Sam, my father's roommate from college who specialized in medical negligence, visited me. I was well enough to leave the hospital with Sam and Dad and dine at a nearby Chinese restaurant. I maneuvered my wheelchair like a pro. I was pleased to discover that the weeks of physical therapy and strengthening my arms had paid off tremendously. I could be independent in this way. I hadn't been to a restaurant in three months, and I immensely appreciated the company. We discussed the possible lawsuit against Dr. Samuels, and even though Sam believed we had a strong case, I was nervous about having to reveal the chaos of my personal life and turmoil over the past seven years. I was demanding thirty million dollars for the doctor's outright negligence that caused me permanent impairments. The doctor's insurance company hired the best team of lawyers to wear me down and get me to relinquish the suit. Although I was insecure about the entire process, I relentlessly sought justice and eventually settled out of court.

I was twenty-eight years old and facing life in a wheelchair. I couldn't run or walk away from my situation. My career as an architect faded. My ambition to be a designer diminished, and I stayed busy with the goals of realizing my physical limitations and finding Mr. Right.

Christmas arrived, and with it came festivities and parties. Mark Hamill of *Star Wars* fame visited the rehab hospital and gave a warm, compelling talk to the patients. I wanted to be up close to him, but an army of wheelchairs surrounded the star, who was doing his best to address everyone equally. Mom and Dad purchased boxes of chocolates for all my aides and nurses as a way of saying, "Thank you."

Then 1985 arrived, and it was time to end my bittersweet journey in the rehab hospital. Dad took me home on a cold day after two months of hard work. I carried the trusty wooden board that helped me transfer my body from the wheelchair to the car seat, and Dad put the wheelchair into the trunk of the car. I bid farewell to my roommate and buddy, Evelyn, knowing we would never cross paths again. Our lives were too different. The ramp my parents had installed at our house made it easy for me to wheel up to the entrance. Mom informed our inquisitive neighbors that the ramp was for tile and lumber deliveries since our bathroom was being renovated. Mom hid my condition from the temple crowd and townspeople. It was difficult for her to cope with the reality of my illness. She did not confide in our rabbi or anyone else, and she didn't want to risk any gossip among our nosy neighbors. She helped me maintain my hygiene. She was generous with her time and devotion and kept her spirits lifted to care for me.

Mom and Dad hired a physical therapist who was active at the rehab hospital. She was committed to helping members of the rehab community. We had physical therapy sessions twice a week in addition to my sessions with George, the psychiatrist recommended by Dr. Chu at the rehab facility. His office was in a wing of his palatial home, thirty minutes away from my parents' house. The waiting room consisted of orange and yellow walls, floor-to-ceiling windows, and French doors. The room also provided a view of a lush garden. Decorative plants were in one corner, and children's books and toys were in the opposite corner. He served hot chocolate, tea, and coffee in this peaceful setting.

From the very beginning of my sessions with George, my parents and brother—when he visited from Colorado—were included in my therapy, which created a supportive bond between us during trying times. In the introductory session, my parents and I outlined the history and events of the prior seven years for George's benefit. The doctor also inquired about my birth and childhood. He took extensive notes while we spoke. Dad had recorded a synopsis of all my meltdowns for George and Sam, the lawyer, to review. My youth consisted of a predisposition to my catastrophic life as a young adult. Signs of my imminent collapse included a severe lack of sleep and burgeoning paranoia of a fictitious reality. These were alerts signaling the need for a support system to catch me before I ran into dangerous situations that could kill me. The doctor diagnosed me as atypical bipolar and continued my daily medicine, Haldol.

George was a Quaker who abstained from drinking. He strongly advised me to stop drinking alcoholic or caffeinated beverages because they could negatively impact my sleep cycle. He also cautioned me not to stretch myself thin with activities. He instructed me to honor the KISS principle, "Keep It Simple Stupid," which meant no more solo trips abroad, no more casual wine, and no more living on the third floor. He had written helpful essays on how to maintain healthy relationships, how to make sound investments, and how to maintain a healthy diet. I felt comfortable opening up to George, and I often lay on his couch and spoke of my thoughts, memories, and dreams.

I told him about the recurring dream that Dr. Samuels never addressed, where I was abandoned and trapped for eternity in a rundown house perched on a cliff that overlooked a desolate valley that once teemed with sea life. In my dream, I wore a long, taupe skirt and white blouse, which was an outfit I wore to temple on the High Holidays. My hair was overgrown and reached to the ground. Squirrels and rats scurried in the decayed structure. As I peered out at the valley below, I saw my brother and John—a student with a dark past I had idolized in my early years of college—walking through the arid desert followed by a line of women with striking blonde hair. John and my brother blatantly preferred dating blondes over brunettes. I was a brunette left in the cold, dank world. I was unattractive to John. George took copious notes about my dream. He discerned that I was suffering from a lonely existence and projecting only the worst for myself in the future. This dream of isolation haunted me through the years as I remained single and without any emotional tie to a mate. George continually advised me not to put "bunions" (a metaphor for obstacles) in my head and to live one day at a time. He encouraged me not to project way into the future. Eventually, his advice got through to me.

My parents hired our maid's husband, Charles, to drive me to George's office twice each week. Charles assisted me as I transferred myself, on my wooden board, from the car to my wheelchair and vice versa. He never inquired about what happened. He accepted me as I was, and I appreciated his assistance. I was comfortable transferring myself from my wheelchair to my bed, the toilet, and the car. It became second nature and a way of life. The possibility of remaining in a wheelchair for the remainder of my life was daunting, but I had to accept that it could be my reality.

My sessions with George provided me with structure and ensured contact with the outside world. I discovered that George was optimistic, and he realized tremendous potential in each person or patient he met. He recognized and encouraged my talents and believed I could successfully establish myself. He was going to help me reach my dreams, realized and unrealized. What more could I want?

CHAPTER 28

Mom accompanied me to my monthly orthopedic appointments. I had not seen the doctor who had operated on me, Dr. Morris, during my stay at the rehab center. The nurse took X-rays of my lower legs and spine so the doctor could determine if my bones were healing and, if so, when the casts could be removed. I used my wooden board to transfer from the wheelchair to the X-ray bed. Each move required an enormous amount of physical effort. I had to lie flat on the table and then turn my entire body sideways so that the X-ray machine could capture different angles of the spine.

Dr. Morris was Irish, like Dr. O'Hara from the rehab center. He had carrot-colored hair and a mustache. He wore bow ties that matched his suits, like George, and often wore his white medical jacket. He seemed tall, but everyone seemed tall from this wheelchair.

I often wondered about Evelyn, my rehab buddy, and what her life was like after her time in the rehab facility. Every patient there suffered from mishaps that impaired a normal life. I promised my mother I would visit the rehab center when I could walk again. I wanted to stumble into Dr. O'Hara since I relentlessly thought about him.

Weeks passed, and I focused on therapy with George, physical therapy, gaining weight, and rekindling friendships. Mom helped me tremendously by assisting with my hygiene and taking me places. Together we developed a sense of humor about my harsh reality.

After three months at home, the time came to remove the casts. Mom took me to see Dr. Morris one morning in the beginning of April 1985. We sat patiently in the crowded waiting room. I felt nervous butterflies and deep anxiety within my gut about whether I would be able to walk again. Since my spinal cord had been nearly severed, I had to adjust to a life of catheterizing myself indefinitely as the question of my mobility hung over me for half a year. The doctor analyzed my X-ray images and, miraculously, determined that my bones and spine were totally healed. After waiting endlessly, the doctor gleefully removed my casts with a small, circular, electric saw. I saw my hairy legs for the first time in five long months. The doctor directed me to stand, and just like that, the moment of truth arrived. I slowly stood up from the chair and noticed that I was a head taller than the gifted doctor. That was the happiest moment of my entire life.

With my arm around his shoulders, I held onto the doctor and slowly took a step. The months of physical therapy helped me, and Dr. Morris was stunned. Mom was relieved and happy for me. I clumsily walked out of that office and left the wheelchair behind. I still had to reestablish my stride, so I continued physical therapy twice a week. I relearned how to navigate stairs. Being so far from the ground was disorienting, and peering down stairwells was disconcerting; therefore, I had to practice descending stairs. I had an uneven gait due to the slight limp that would never recede. I couldn't stand on my tippy toes, do a backbend, jog, or run, but I could walk. I continued wearing my torso brace for four more months.

During the five months I had been in a wheelchair, Morty somehow convinced Mom, Dad, and me that he would take care of my apartment and car during my long absence. After I was walking again, I took everything back into my possession and locked him out of the apartment. He was angry that he had to vacate, but I could not have cared less. He was jobless during those five months, and he used my half of our joint bank account for his trip to Florida and his living expenses while in my apartment. The amount he usurped was $3,000.

But Morty was still in my life. In May 1985, we went to see the Woody Allen film *The Purple Rose of Cairo*. A long line waited outside the movie theater, so Morty summoned the manager and informed him of my handicap. I was still wearing the torso brace and using a cane. The manager was skeptical, so Morty knocked on my torso brace to prove I had spinal cord injuries and therefore could not stand for long periods of time. The manager allowed us to skip the line, but I don't remember if Morty paid for my ticket.

Morty and I were not living together, but he still wanted to have sex with no strings attached. I figured he thought of me as an easy target. Part of me struggled to deny him, because I was falling into my old habit of believing there was more to our vacuous relationship. I mustered my strength and did not succumb to his selfish, opportunist, and noncommittal intentions. I was not attracted to him anymore, and I finally realized his motives of using me and that we had no future. The torso brace helped keep me in check when I felt weak, as it hindered me from pursuing sexual activities for some time. I stopped all communication with Morty. I thought I could give him a second chance, but his insincere motives became blatant when he wanted to have sex. It was finally over, and I had to move on with my life.

Before I reentered the workforce, Mom and I visited the rehab hospital. I wore a stunning charcoal-gray tweed jacket and midlength skirt. I strived to look beautiful and mesmerize Dr. O'Hara, the iconic figure of my thoughts, the doctor who permeated my soul. We strolled to the second floor and peered into my old room. I realized Evelyn was gone, but the cruel South African aide who had treated her so shabbily was still there. We had no words for each other, only mutual contempt.

We walked to the hospital cafeteria, and Dr. O'Hara appeared suddenly. He greeted me coolly and contained his reaction to seeing me standing with a cane. He asked me to walk a small distance, and he was quietly amazed but rather curt. The doctor inquired what I was doing with my time now that I was walking again. I proudly informed him that I was seeking work in the field of architecture, and I might be hired to design a house for a potential client. He did not seem impressed. Perhaps he thought my profession was not a viable and healthy choice for someone with my mental condition. I felt disappointed and suddenly yearned to become a nurse and be part of his world. I found it impossible to impress the doctor with my beauty or profession.

The doctor briskly wished me good luck, then continued on his way. I turned to my mother, who witnessed the cold interaction. She could see my disappointment. My main reason for visiting the hospital was to see the man I had idolized for the past five months. It was a tremendous letdown that he had no enthusiasm for me. My fantasies painted us in sweet conversation and potentially planning for a date, but Dr. O'Hara treated me like a second-class citizen, someone who was still broken by mental strife and could never live up to his standards. Despite his rejection, my boundless feelings for him had enabled me to survive the many months in a wheelchair. Now, I had to forget him and move on to explore new relationships.

I resumed my life with fervor. I applied for a drafting position at a local architect's office. It was a small family business, and the boss's son hoarded all the interesting drafting tasks. Two other skilled draftsmen worked there as well. The boss's wife was the receptionist and bookkeeper. I became part of the team of serious employees: Barry, who was from Egypt; Sam, who was from Lebanon; and Al, the boss's son. They were all nice-looking men I felt attracted to. I was persistent in my search to find a soul mate, my partner for a lifetime. This remained my underlying motive wherever I sought employment. The office had only two rooms. The receptionist welcomed people, and the boss convened with potential clients in the front room. The drafters worked in the back room with the blueprint copier machine.

One evening, Sam and I visited Barry at his tiny studio apartment in the heart of Queens. Since Sam and Barry were both foreigners, they lived in humble but adequate apartments as they attempted to make a viable living in the United States. As soon as we arrived at Barry's, I rushed to the bathroom because I couldn't control my bowels. I was partially paralyzed, so my colon sphincter was lax. Sam and Barry had no idea about my condition. I parked on Barry's toilet for twenty long minutes. I was anxious and feared making a spectacle of myself. Sometimes I eliminated in my pants while driving to various activities and had to return home to change my soiled garments. I was lucky I never had a mishap in a very public place.

Sam, Barry, and I dined in a Chinese restaurant that was a short walk from Barry's apartment. The three of us walked arm in arm as we flirted with one another and thoroughly enjoyed our relaxed dynamics. We worked together and respected each other. Dinner was inexpensive and satisfying. I lived at home with my parents, thus forgoing the experience of living on a modest paycheck, unlike Sam and Barry, whose families were halfway across the globe. They were hard workers, though, and determined to make America their home. Our boss was generous enough to sponsor Barry and Sam when they applied for green cards. Over time, they became responsible citizens.

CHAPTER 29

My attraction to the men at work grew as each day passed. I had also reestablished my communication with Roger. He never found out about my devastating accident, and we decided to get together often. He had moved from Manhattan to a quaint apartment in a two-story brick building in the Bronx. We dined at fine restaurants, and I frequently stayed the night at his apartment, though our relationship never extended beyond its platonic state. Our friendship lasted for several years following college, but eventually it died, because I wanted more than Roger could give. He never inquired about my slight limp or my long absence during my convalescence. Instead, he always regarded me as the same beauty he initially dated during the first six months of our relationship, when we shared love, passion, and adoration for each other.

George led group therapy once a week. These sessions took place in the waiting room of his office. The group consisted of five male patients and me. We varied in age, and all were established in their professions except for Gary, who was the youngest in the group, and me.

Gary worked for his wealthy father. He was boisterous and outspoken. Everyone suggested Gary branch out and work for other employers instead of being so dependent on his father. Gary also drove an expensive car that his father had given him. Tim, a successful orthopedist, remarked that he had never driven an expensive car until he stood on his own two feet. He stated that, even though his father was wealthy, he did not rely so heavily on him. Everyone agreed, and this offended Gary, who eventually took his anger out on me, citing his inability to communicate with me as a reason to leave the group.

Paul, a financier, consistently complained that he couldn't stomach the way his wife smelled and was contemplating abandoning her. Even after being together for so long, his wife apparently had no idea Paul felt that way. We all advised Paul not to act impulsively but to try to communicate his feelings to his wife.

Ed, who was a research scientist, perpetually grieved over the death of a stranger he accidentally ran over while driving. Despite the passage of many years, the accident festered like a fresh wound in Ed's psyche and burdened his entire existence.

Meanwhile, Tim, the successful orthopedist, confided to the group that two or three times a year he was crippled by extreme anxiety. He curled up in a fetal position and remained frozen for three days. Tim was desperate to resolve his illness since it frightened his wife and young children.

Sal, who was also a financier, spent all his money carelessly, and his wife was losing patience with him as she tried to guide him away from bankruptcy and financial ruin.

Then there was me. I told the group I had been in a serious accident, but I did not confess how or why it happened. I boldly admitted that I had to self-administer my catheter, and based on my brief revelations, Tim surmised that I had fallen a distance. While I was slightly ashamed that he had guessed part of the truth, I felt proud that I had endured more than most people my age. I was disappointed that the group hardly acknowledged my great feat of survival. They were too consumed with their own troubles. And I don't think they took me seriously, perhaps because I was the only woman in the group.

I contacted an outspoken woman I had met in the gym before my fall. She was eight years my senior, and her son was ten years younger than me. Marge was gregarious and ambitious. She lived with her husband in the same town where I experienced my devastating fall, and she was employed in the garment district of Manhattan. I showed a lot of resilience by returning to the town where my accident occurred and by seeking a friendship with a mere acquaintance. Marge and I eventually forged a strong bond, and we cherished our friendship. She did not question my seven-month disappearance, and I hid my "dark side" from her.

When summer arrived, Marge and I visited the beach at Hempstead Harbor. I struggled to walk on the sand and sit on the towel, so Marge helped me stand erect when it was time to leave. We dined at a yacht club café and devoured scrumptious baked clams. Our conversations often alluded to how vile Morty had been. Privately, I thought to myself that very few men could tolerate living with me as my dangerous breakdowns persisted, and understanding my cyclic illness was trying.

Even though I was finally free of unhealthy relationships, and my friendship with Marge helped me overcome my low self-esteem, I remained alone and couldn't imagine a man being attracted to me and my chaotic existence. Marge was encouraging and always asserted that Mr. Right would appear one day, but she didn't know that Mr. Right would have to accept my breakdowns and mental illness too. Marge often saw Morty while commuting on the train to Manhattan. He finally got a job as a judge in traffic court. She commented on how seedy he appeared while carrying a broken briefcase.

The fall of 1985 came and went, and I stayed with my job at the local architect's office. I whistled while I worked, which, unbeknownst to me, distracted others. I found myself once again frustrated with the unimportant tasks assigned and restless to do and be more. Despite my frustration, I was taken with my coworkers. The boss was aware of my mediocre work habits, but I don't think he cared, as he enjoyed my buoyant personality.

I still lived with my parents, and I continued my physical therapy sessions. I worked on strengthening the muscles in my legs, compensating for the nerve damage on my left side that caused my uneven gait. I was impressed with my physical therapist, who was a tall, statuesque brunette, both diligent and caring. I gifted her a pair of boots just because I admired her so much. She accepted them, although she acted as though she thought it was awkward since there was no occasion for giving gifts. Meanwhile, I spent my available time shopping for clothes that flattered my tall hourglass figure. Shopping became an expensive hobby, but it was beneficial for my self-esteem. The boss's wife showered me with compliments about how beautiful I looked, and those remarks became part of my survival.

CHAPTER 30

George continued to prescribe a low, daily dose of Haldol. It made me want to crawl out of my skin, but I believed it helped reduce the number of breakdowns I suffered. George also prescribed Cogentin, a drug that addressed the jittery side effects of the Haldol. Cogentin hardly made a difference, but I continued taking it, hoping it would be effective.

In the spring of 1986, I started to look for an apartment. I wanted to live independently again and thought it would be more attractive to a potential mate if I lived on my own. George instructed me to consider ground-floor apartments, but they were unaffordable in the town where my co-op was located. I changed my search some and considered living in a town adjacent to my hometown, which had hilly avenues and narrow streets lined with Victorian-style houses. I eventually found an apartment on the second floor of a picturesque period house.

Meanwhile, I looked for a different job and discovered an opportunity to work for a local interior designer. The owner of the company, a tall, debonair man, studied my portfolio of building designs from college and determined I would be capable of designing a lingerie store for a demanding client. The empty interior space for the store was an awkward size, elongated and not very wide, about twenty-five-by-one-hundred feet. I had a vision of how to effectively design and furnish the space, and the owner hired me immediately for the project. I left my job at the small architect's office on good terms.

The new firm was also small, so I worked with only two fellow employees. Jane was well-endowed, married, and pregnant with her third child. I wanted to be a parent. I was thirty years old, and my biological clock was ticking. At the time, it seemed impossible for me to start a family, so I envied Jane. She was so far ahead of me in the game of life.

Bob was about my height and had chestnut hair and an olive complexion. I was not attracted to him, but we established a good working relationship. Bob and Jane had worked at the firm together for several years. Since they had seniority, I was allocated the task of making blueprints when needed and designing the awkward space that no one could imagine turning into a viable store. Completing the design took me about three weeks. I created a dynamic design that enhanced the linear space, and I implemented a curved soffit from the ceiling, that spanned the length of the space and three quarters of the width. Visually, the soffit split the space into two parts and created an illusion of a wider space. I designed decorative columns that together defined the space. Under the curved soffit, displays of lingerie hung, and in the back of the store, where the ceiling ended, dressing rooms were designed. The wall opposite the soffit was comprised of compartments defined by minicolumns and arches, where undergarments were displayed. The entire design was inspired by the Acropolis of Athens.

The two-dimensional drawings I created for the design were second rate. The curved soffit that I translated to the drawing was uneven. My boss and Bob admonished me for an amateur, unprofessional drawing of my engaging design. Unfortunately, despite being a solid designer, I wasn't the world's best draftsman. I sat by my drafting desk amid the tight office quarters for three weeks, creating and drafting my design. Soon after I completed the drawings for the lingerie store, the owner abruptly fired me. I was shocked. How could I be fired? The boss must have hired me to design the challenging space so he could finish the project and then remove me from his payroll. I was flustered because I had fulfilled design requirements that no one else in the office could achieve. I knew I was a competent designer, but it was time to reevaluate my direction and purpose.

I ran into Bob years later, and he informed me that the firm closed due to the boss's cocaine addiction. This made some sense at least.

In the spring of 1986, I moved into my apartment in the Victorian house, and my brother retired from the army. One of the most important reasons he opted for civilian life was that he wanted to find a Jewish woman to settle down with and start a family. I wanted to help him, so I threw a party to welcome him home and invited friends and family to attend. I invited an acquaintance I knew from synagogue and my days in public school. Her name was Roz, same as our grandmother. She was petite and gracious. She had thick, curly hair and came from a family of eight siblings. Her parents' home was about two miles east of our parents' house. Roz was living in the city and studying law, and she was eager to meet my brother. I believed they were perfectly suited for each other.

The guest list included a few friends from college and camp days, cousins, Marge, a few people from work, and Gary from my therapy group. I introduced Gary to my cousin, and their meeting flourished into a marriage two years later. Gary and I eventually had it out because he believed I violated his privacy during group. I mentioned my cousin's bathroom renovation in her apartment in the city and said I had heard it was beautiful. Gary saw this as a breach of privacy and abandoned the group on a sour note. He used this isolated incident as an excuse to stop seeing George as well. Due to his angry behavior, I kept my distance from him after that.

My brother didn't connect with anyone at the party, so about two weeks later, we attended a Jewish singles event at an upscale lounge in New York City. As we sat at the bar, we noticed a well-dressed, pretty lady sitting alone at a cocktail table. My brother was shy, so I gave him a pep talk that highlighted his success as a handsome Jewish man, retired as a major in the military, with a nice apartment and prospects of owning Dad's business. My brother and the pretty lady married two years later. Everyone in my life was being paired up through my efforts, but it was time for me to find a man for myself.

After a discussion with George, Mom, and Dad about my direction in the job market, I took a hiatus from architecture and interior design firms. I returned to my father's business to work as an estimator and draftsman. I was lonely living by myself with only Ming Lee for company. On one of our walks, I befriended a woman who lived several blocks from me. Her name was Felicia. She was about fifty years old, had three grown children, and was divorced. She lived in a top-floor apartment in another Victorian-style house. Felicia invited me over for a cup of coffee, and I confided in her. I told her I had trouble finding a man to have a lasting relationship with, and I had to face living alone for the rest of my days. Felicia gave me a small book of the New Testament to comfort my poor state of mind. That portion of the Bible was not included in my faith, but I graciously accepted her kind gift.

I placed an ad in the singles column in *New York Magazine* and received a response. I mailed the stranger a photo of myself holding my little dog. He immediately responded, and I invited him to my apartment. He was Israeli and drove a broken-down car despite being an engineer. As we sat together in my kitchen, we conversed easily. I found myself attracted to his deep voice. After several dates, I made the grave error of inviting this man of mystery to my parents' home. He immediately assumed I was wealthy. When he saw my parents' beautifully furnished house on the water's edge, he saw dollar signs.

Then he made a mistake by inviting me to his extremely run-down apartment in Brooklyn. His living situation reminded me too much of my relationship with Morty, and I wasn't sure what my counterpart had to offer. I wasn't even sure I believed he was an engineer. I let the relationship fade.

Meanwhile, my stepcousin was planning her summer wedding. She invited me without an escort, and when I asked if I could bring a guest, she responded that we had to be seriously involved. Then she quickly remarked that she had no more room on her guest list. I attended the wedding alone. My family, cousins, and brother were all paired with their serious partners. They ignored me the entire time.

The wedding took place in an elegant restaurant on a pier overlooking the East River in Manhattan. The reception and cocktail room gave spectacular views of the river and the Brooklyn Bridge. The ambiance was the only thing I enjoyed because I felt awkward, alone, and out of place. During the reception, I sat with my brother and his girlfriend, my cousins, and an obnoxious, single man with whom I danced exactly once. I left the wedding with my parents shortly after the main course. When I got up from my chair, I noticed blood on the cushion. I quickly pushed the chair under the table and prayed no one noticed the red mark. I made a hasty excuse about leaving for Florida the next morning and then left with my parents.

Dad decided to sell his building in Brooklyn and move his office. He delegated the task of finding a new building to me. This became my work for the next several months, as I searched with diligence and the aid of real estate agents from Brooklyn and Queens. I examined vacant warehouses in dangerous areas, and after months of searching, discovered a building in a semi-industrial area close to New York City and in the vicinity of the Brooklyn-Queens Expressway. I was organized in my search. I made a checklist for each building I visited, and I kept my father informed of my progress. Location was a prominent consideration. The new building was not far from a subway that led to New York City, and it was close to the highway trucks would use to deliver supplies.

Vinny, an archie student from my past and someone I saw several times over the years, started visiting me on weekends. He traveled from Albany, where he lived, just to see me. We arrived at a crossroad in our relationship when I questioned the seriousness of our affair. We had known each other for years—were we serious enough to get married? As soon as I expressed this to Vinny, he backed away and said he didn't love me. His confession burned my soul, and after several weeks passed, Vinny sent me a letter. He emphasized that he made a mistake in ending our years of friendship and romance. I ignored his words and continued my life without him. He couldn't take back his injurious words. The damage had already been done.

CHAPTER 31

I hired a dating service for a year, which cost me six hundred dollars. Wendy, the matchmaker, who was amiable and loaded with positive energy, assembled an attractive profile describing my individuality. I kept my dark side a secret while describing myself as a successful architect working in a related field. I informed Wendy of my interests, which included classical music, fine art, and skiing. She took a flattering photo of me to add to my profile.

I met a handsome man named Mark, who was tall and graceful. He had vivid blue eyes, bushy black hair, and a fair complexion. Mark hesitated to describe his profession. He worked for his father, who owned and managed several beauty schools on Long Island. He had a disabled sister who became the source of discord between his divorced parents. Mark was smitten with me and found it hard to believe that I was attracted to him. We ate at inexpensive restaurants and kissed in the park at night. He showed me his apartment. He had only a queen-sized mattress on his bedroom floor.

Mark had a volatile life, and his father was highly critical of him. I introduced Mark and his father to George, who arranged to have one therapy session with the troubled pair. After meeting with them, George cautioned me that Mark and his family were not marriage material, and I should consider moving on to a different prospect. Despite George's warning, I continued my relationship with Mark since I was drawn to his good looks and gentle manner. I brushed aside his father's sentiments of guilt, remorse, disappointment, and spite that interfered with his family functioning in a healthy way. Mark's father had relinquished any responsibility for his disabled daughter, and Mark's mother took care of her alone. I invited Mark to my apartment, and we became physically intimate. In the morning, while I was busy preparing for work, Mark attempted to cook an egg in the microwave. The egg exploded, and he could have broken my microwave. This made me realize Mark was not responsible enough to be in a relationship, and what he sought from me was security and stability. It was a one-way street, as I was Mark's therapist. I instructed him in the KISS principle that George had taught me. I suggested he concentrate on establishing a routine, improving his performance at work, and making his apartment a comforting place where he could have peace of mind.

After several weeks of Mark's absence, he called me. He was in a psych ward at a private hospital. I attempted to visit him but was barred from entering since I had been a patient there numerous times. I found it astonishing that, for once, I was on the other side of the locked door.

I felt sorry that I could not be there for Mark. The entire situation seemed ironic.

In the meantime, Dad hired an architect to design the interior office space of his new building. When the architect completed the design, I examined the two-dimensional drawings. I found the design failed to create an open space and was confining and narrow in its scope. I told my father that I could enhance the design. He agreed. I repositioned my father's office, an additional office on the north side, and three more offices on the west side. In the remaining area, open cubicles housed secretaries, the bookkeeper, and the accountant. The south side of the open space contained drafting desks, the blueprint copier, large filing cabinets, and an area for the estimator. Four large skylights lit the open space. My father heartily approved the new design and its inspirational organization of open space. The architect expedited my design, and he integrated the heating and cooling systems to accommodate with the dramatic ceiling. I worked on the design of my father's new building for a month or two, and I began to feel good about my work since I was being challenged and implementing my creativity and energy.

I was through with the men I had dated, pined over, or was attracted to. I threw out to the universe: Joseph, Jack, John, Roy, Bill, Roger, Vinny, Ron, Doug, Pascal, Morty, Sam, Barry, and the nameless Israeli. Before my intent could become reality Ron phoned me out of the blue and invited himself to my apartment. I was innocently flattered that he did not forget me. He took the train in from Brooklyn, and I met him at the station.

As soon as I let him into the apartment and we sat down in my comfortable living room, he started making sexual advances. Suddenly, this religious man from my past was attempting to have sex with me. He was a virgin, and he desperately wanted to experience sex without any attachment with someone from outside his holy restrictive circle.

I told him, in no uncertain terms, that if we had sex we would have to marry, and I wouldn't mind living a religious life. Ron was shocked by the demand and insisted I would not be welcome in the religious community. I refused to have sex with him, and I took him back to his train and said goodbye for the last time. He considered me a whore he could use for experience without establishing a commitment. I was simply an "inferior woman" he could use and then dispose of and forget. Damn him!

I continued my sessions with George, and I told him about a dream that occurred shortly after my revelation of breaking with the men in my life and forging ahead alone. On a rocky peninsula stood a bride who was wearing a voluminous, white lace gown and long veil. The bride was a man with a face like Freud. He wore a bold, intricate, emerald necklace and dangling, emerald earrings. He peered into the wilderness as if he expected a hidden creature to come forth. George said the dream signified that I stood at a rocky turning point in my life. I was new (symbolized by the green jewelry in my dreams) to pursuing a meaningful beginning. He suggested I might turn to fine art and engage in painting.

Marge introduced me to an art studio about a mile from where I had my accident. The two-story studio housed twenty artists who rented ten-by-ten-foot spaces. I rented space on the lower floor and began my career as an artist. Most of the artists' styles followed the abstract school. An older artist painted floral landscapes and sold them. The artists were women in their fifties and sixties, and most were married with grown children. Only one artist was close to my age. She was married to a psychologist and had a ten-year-old boy. The artists were nurturing and good at listening. I often spoke of my quest to be an artist, while questioning how one could thrive economically in this pursuit.

I felt comfortable painting, as though I had pursued that activity my entire life. For a short time, I tried painting in the abstract style. I was harnessing my imagination, and by having somewhere to travel other than my apartment or my father's office, I felt at home in the studio. It became a special place for me.

I had choices. I could become a social worker, a career I was well-suited for due to my own personal experiences. This required more schooling, though, which was a displeasing thought. I could return to the field of architecture, or I could do something different. I felt positive vibes about my life and was influenced by George's optimism. He always remarked, "Opportunity knocks and knocks."

CHAPTER 32

Fall passed, and the dead of winter arrived. I was single and alone. I sought solace and peace, striving to be content with myself. Regardless of my achievements and George's optimism, I still felt inadequate. Earning my degree in architecture took seven years of struggle. I didn't achieve good grades and failed in my senior design presentation, so I had to repeat it in the summer of 1981. According to my harsh opinion of myself, I wasn't good enough. I undermined my accomplishments and was immensely critical of myself.

Instead of taking it a day, an hour, or a moment at a time, I peered thirty years into the future, imagining a bleak, desolate world, and felt lonely and desperate. This habitual projection causing immense despair led to the onset of my breakdowns and manifested into a cycle of a delusional reality. I wasn't consciously aware that I had to change the voice inside my head. I had to break this pattern of personal destruction, which took years of struggle and George's guidance.

Out of the blue, the dating service called and informed me that a man was interested in meeting me. I was surprised and skeptical, but I finally agreed to meet him. He came to my apartment, and when we exchanged salutations, he nervously called me Rita. It was an awkward moment. I corrected him and told him my name was Ruth. Tinged with embarrassment, he introduced himself as Richard. I invited him in for a tour of my apartment.

Richard wore a brown corduroy suit, and his face was a mix between Freud and Groucho Marx. He looked like the bride in the optimistic dream I told George about. Richard was half an inch taller than me. I wore snow boots with no heels since the forecast called for snow that evening of February 20, 1987. I wore a pink angora sweater that hid my breasts and a long, gray, wool-blend skirt. Initially, we searched for words, but as the evening progressed, we developed a positive rapport. I did not know what religion Richard was, but it didn't matter. I was keen on finding a sincere, compassionate, understanding, well-mannered, and thoughtful individual. I knew it was a tall order, which was why I had given up my search for Mr. Right.

I showed Richard the peaceful view of the harbor from the bay window in my living room. The harbor was visible since the trees had shed their leaves. Richard was quiet and appreciated the ambiance of my apartment. He was surprised to see my queen-size, Ralph Lauren bed that dominated my modestly sized bedroom. Possibilities swirled in our heads as we made polite conversation on our way to the restaurant ten miles away. Navigating the roads was difficult since the ground was slippery with snow and we were traveling in Richard's sports car.

I felt shy and unsure about how to broaden our conversation. At the restaurant, Richard consumed a small glass of sherry and informed me that he attended medical school in Bologna, Italy. His father had attended the school as well, just before the outbreak of World War II. Richard was seeking his residency, and he planned to specialize in psychiatry. He had lived in Italy for eight years and considered making it his home, but something compelled him to return to America. Although he spoke Italian fluently, he still felt his inescapable identity as an American. The fact that Richard wanted to be a psychiatrist and I considered being a social worker led me to believe we had a lot in common. Richard didn't notice my uneven gait, or, if he did, was polite enough not to mention it. His sincerity and manners overshadowed all the men I had dated in the past. Somehow, I felt that my meeting with Richard was unique and serendipitous.

As we conversed, I learned that Richard didn't have any siblings, and most of his family perished in World War II. He was alone, and I sensed he wanted to build connections with other people. I yearned to reveal my troubled past to him, but I was deterred by the fact that it was our first date. There would be time to explain later. Dinner came to an end, and Richard drove us back and parked his car in front of my apartment. He opened my car door and kissed my cheek. We said goodbye to a romantic evening. Richard drove back to his parents' home in Queens, which was about an hour from where I lived. As I watched his car fade into the snowy distance, I had no idea whether we would have a second date.

The stress of winter and dating again pierced my peace of mind. My fears resurfaced, and I could not control my increasing paranoia. I experienced a miniscule breakdown. I was outside of myself, crawling out of my thin skin and deeply entwined in an illusory world. I managed to go to work at my father's office without anyone noticing my agitated state, but I struggled to hold myself together. George advised me to increase my Haldol dosage. While I managed to avoid a major breakdown and the psych ward, a cloud of uncertainty engulfed me. Where was I going? When would my reality improve? Is divine intervention plausible? When would I face and resolve my fears? I used every bit of strength I had to survive.

A few days melted away, then Richard called me. I felt a moment of elation during a time of suffering. He inquired about having dinner together again, and I agreed. When Richard arrived at my apartment for the second time, he called me by the right name. I was quiet and said few words. I was anxious and held onto a thin thread of sanity, but I found Richard's presence comforting. This time we ate nearby at an Indian restaurant. I let Richard do all the talking, and I only spoke enough to ask brief questions about the topics he introduced. I hoped my anxiety-ridden condition was masked and he judged me as a good listener. He couldn't possibly imagine the frenzied state I was in. We finally left the restaurant at eleven when it closed, and I was surprised that our date lasted so long, despite my unnerving silence.

He kissed my cheek again, and as I stood out in the cold, watching his car fade into the darkness, I wondered if he would call me again and disregard my pensive behavior that evening. I climbed the stairs to my apartment and turned in for the night. I was able to sleep since the Haldol kept my thoughts from racing. Slowly, my small breakdown was retreating, and I managed to keep my daily routine and care for Ming Lee.

The week passed slowly, and I hoped Richard would call me again. The universe heard my silent wishes, and Richard asked if I would see a movie with him. The third time's a charm, as they say, and I discovered I was comfortable with Richard. I could trust him, and I took the plunge and revealed my maladies to him. I told him about my accident, and he remained calm and unexpressive. Nothing seemed to faze him. He either brushed my truths to the sidelines or did not realize the seriousness of my condition. Maybe he had never met someone with a mental illness, or maybe he was surprised by my honesty.

We saw a gory movie titled *Angel Heart*. We made out during the entire movie. The patrons behind us complained that we were distracting them from their view of the screen, but we didn't let them spoil our fun. No more kisses on the cheek—the wheels of passion were set in motion. Richard and I both were in awe of our newly established relationship. I told him more about my past, and he never judged me. We both felt the potential growing between us. We were a couple, and as we approached intimacy, I informed Richard that we would need to be serious enough to consider marriage if we were to consummate our relationship. In late March, Richard got down on his knee and asked me to be his bride. My lifelong search had been fulfilled. I said yes. I felt like I had known Richard all my life.

Richard moved into my apartment. We were full of bliss, planning a future together. We planned to get married on the first day of summer, exactly four months after we met. I met his parents at an Italian restaurant in the heart of Queens. Richard and I both were nervous about the introduction. His parents were reserved and conservative. I learned quickly that they were survivors of the Holocaust. They had been imprisoned in a camp in Italy, Ferramonti, until the end of World War II. They lived in the camp for many years, and every prisoner stationed there survived. After the war, Richard's parents lived together for three years and finally married in Rome.

Richard's father came from a northeastern town in Poland on the border of Russia. In 1939, he failed a course at the medical school and subsequently had to repeat the course in the summer when Germany invaded Poland. While he was retaking the course in Italy, his family and relatives were murdered. Because he was a Jew, he was transported to Ferramonti until the end of the war; he was despondent and powerless to save his family from death.

Meanwhile, Richard's mother returned home one day in Yugoslavia to find that her parents and first husband had been taken to death camps and slaughtered by the Nazis. She hastily packed her bag with photos of her family and her grandmother's diamond earrings and fled Yugoslavia with her brother-in-law. They walked through the Southern Alps into Italy and were eventually deported to Ferramonti, where she met Richard's father.

Richard's parents looked at me with curiosity and noticed my limp. Richard's father asked why I had an uneven gait, and Richard simply told them it was from an accident. He guarded my privacy and my dignity. He finally informed his parents that we were engaged. They met this announcement with shock and doubt since it was a lot to process all at once.

I introduced Richard to my parents, my brother, and his girlfriend, Carol, at a local restaurant. When Richard said he aspired to be a psychiatrist, I could tell they were impressed. Richard and I sat close together and held hands under the table as we waited for the right moment to announce our engagement. A space in the conversation opened, and we revealed our exciting news. It hit my parents like a ton of bricks. After all the years of struggle, this was finally happening. Their happiness surfaced, and everyone at the table congratulated us with light enthusiasm.

Richard commenced his residency at the hospital in Staten Island. At the end of April, we moved to an apartment closer to his place of work. I was lonely, living so far from my family and friends, but I kept working in Brooklyn and commuting to the art studio in Long Island. When I got pregnant with our first child, Richard wanted to make our union legal immediately. The mayor of Glen Cove married us on May 28, 1987. We celebrated by having dinner in a quaint Italian restaurant with Dad. Unfortunately, my mother was sick and unable to attend. Soon after the dinner, Richard and I informed Mom and

Dad that I was pregnant, and they were worried about the unknown future.

Everything happened so fast that I did not have time to realize the enormous changes coming in my life. My dreams became a reality, and George's optimism prevailed. I was married to a man who was sincere, honest, and compassionate. I was in love and pregnant.

Mom and I planned my official religious wedding, which was to take place in the temple where my parents were members and where I attended Hebrew school in my youth. The temple was cost effective and available, which was important since we planned the wedding in a brief amount of time. Mom and I went shopping for my wedding dress. I found the dress of my dreams at a well-known bridal shop in Brooklyn. The dress was European, and it was discounted since it was meant for another wedding that had been canceled. The top of the gown was formfitting and covered with sequins. The bottom was a flowing skirt of chiffon. The top fell off my shoulders and had a ruffle bordering the edges. It was elegant and romantic. Despite being pregnant and having morning sickness, I was still thin and able to fit into the size 10 gown. I was nervous about getting sick and vomiting during our wedding, which would tip people off that I was pregnant. Richard and I did not want to reveal that yet. My parents were the only ones who knew, and they were worried all of this would lead me to another mental breakdown.

Richard and I hired a twelve-piece band and had a conference with the rabbi, who was disappointed that we were already legally married. We never told him why we rushed into a legal union. My mother hired a caterer and arranged for beautiful floral ensembles for the chuppah, the place in the synagogue where Richard and I were to exchange vows. Richard's parents paid for the grouping of flowers that would adorn each dinner table in the ballroom. My engagement ring was designed by an established jeweler and created in a classical setting, with Richard's great-grandmother's diamonds set on each side of a sapphire stone. At Passover dinner, which was a tradition at Richard's parents' home, I showed off my engagement ring to all the guests. Every guest was a Holocaust survivor and lived near Richard's parents. I felt honored to be among survivors of the worst carnage in human history. My engagement ring was a symbol of peace and survival, and I would never part with it. We sent invitations to one hundred seventy-five people, including family, coworkers, family friends, and buddies from childhood.

Following Passover, my brother's girlfriend, Carol, and my mother planned a surprise shower for me. Richard tried to keep it a surprise, but I knew when he took me to the restaurant on Long Island that something was planned. When I walked into the restaurant, the women in my life greeted me with excitement and eagerness to celebrate. I visited each table of guests and thanked the ladies for their generosity. After our meal, everyone sat in a circle around me as I opened their gifts, which included fancy baskets of soaps and creams, picture frames, a coffee maker, crystal vases, and a white satin nightgown with matching robe. It was a happy event, and I relished being the center of attention.

The night before our wedding, Richard and I slept at our respective parents' homes. I had waited decades and desired this all my life. The special day finally arrived, and I couldn't eat a thing. I wasn't sick, which was great, but I was excited and anxious. This was my moment to shine with hope and happiness for a bright future. I got dressed slowly as everyone in the house prepared for the day. My grandparents, though aged and frail, were visiting. And they were thrilled to see their granddaughter betrothed.

The day was cloudy with a slight drizzle but no humidity. We arrived at the temple early to rehearse the ceremony. Richard wore a gray tuxedo that illuminated his green eyes and complimented my attire. The photographer stayed busy. Reva, my camp friend from long ago, and Richard's best man, also a camp friend, signed our Ketubah, a religious marriage contract. The Ketubah was artfully created with special Hebrew script by my second cousin, who made personal Ketubahs for Jewish weddings.

The guests arrived, and the synagogue slowly filled with our relatives and friends. Carol was my maid of honor, and her three-year-old adorable daughter slowly walked down the center aisle, tossing rose petals. Carol and the best man stood by the chuppah, waiting for the ceremony to begin. Then Richard's parents escorted him down the aisle and stopped before the stairs leading up to the chuppah. Richard ascended the stairs. My parents escorted me down the aisle, and we stopped before the stairs. Richard motioned to my father to escort me up the stairs to meet him. Then my father motioned to Richard to descend the stairs and fetch me. This futile motioning continued back and forth for a nerve-wracking minute. Everyone laughed. Finally, Richard descended the stairs and escorted me to the chuppah. We exchanged our vows and committed to love each other through sickness, health, happy times, and meltdowns!

Ever since that arctic night in Jamaica Bay, when I felt my left hand warmed by an angel, I hoped for commitment. Now that hand was adorned with a gold band of peace. One journey was complete, and a new one was just beginning.